Praise for

Your Money Has Feelings

"Money doesn't grow on trees, but it sure does grow in our minds and imagination. Shannon Ryan lifts the hood on our inner lives that form our often-complicated relationship with money. By fusing her own vulnerability and professional expertise, Ryan crafts a powerful cocktail to combat economic anxiety. This book guides a path toward a financial roadmap via personal anecdotes. Filled with engaging reflections and prompts, *Your Money Has Feelings* is a must-read for anyone with nagging emotions around finances—in other words, it's all of us!"

—**Heather Hach Hearne,** screenwriter of *Freaky Friday*
and book writer for *Legally Blonde the Musical*

"What separates Shannon Ryan's book from those I've read in the past is her ability to provide advice by bringing the reader inside important and very emotional human stories. The writing is clear, engaging, and not a financial boilerplate."

—**Tom Sullivan,** singer, actor, writer, and motivational speaker

"I loved reading this book. As I read each story of real people who overcame fears that blocked their financial happiness, I saw my parents, my friends and myself. Not everyone overcomes their fears. Shannon shares some of those stories, too. This book points the way, honestly. It has spurred some very healthy and fruitful money conversations among my family, friends, and with my own financial advisor."

—**Eliza Mountcastle Shah,** PhD, executive coach, and business owner

YOUR MONEY HAS FEELINGS

UNDERSTAND YOUR FINANCIAL WOUNDS
TO FIND TRUE FREEDOM

YOUR
MONEY
HAS
FEELINGS

SHANNON RYAN, CFP®

GREENLEAF
BOOK GROUP PRESS

Published by Greenleaf Book Group Press
Austin, Texas
www.gbgpress.com

Distributed by Greenleaf Book Group

For ordering information or special discounts for bulk purchases, please
contact Greenleaf Book Group at PO Box 91869, Austin, TX 78709,
512.891.6100.

Design and composition by Greenleaf Book Group
Cover design by Greenleaf Book Group
Cover image used under license from ©stock.adobe.com/creativesunday

Publisher's Cataloging-in-Publication data is available.

Print ISBN: 979-8-88645-384-3

eBook ISBN: 979-8-88645-393-5

To offset the number of trees consumed in the printing of our books,
Greenleaf donates a portion of the proceeds from each printing to the
Arbor Day Foundation. Greenleaf Book Group has replaced over
50,000 trees since 2007.

Printed in the United States of America on acid-free paper

25 26 27 28 29 30 31 32   10 9 8 7 6 5 4 3 2 1

First Edition

Contents

Foreword

The literary marketplace is overloaded and weighed down by books that are supposed to teach you everything you need to know to achieve financial independence and security. They offer formulas, charts, and statistics that suggest if you implement the data found in their pages, you will reach your financial goals and live a long, happy, and productive life. I'm not suggesting that they are wrong; in fact, my Alexa library has some wonderful titles that have benefited my wife, Patty, and me as we've traveled along our financial journey.

What separates Shannon Ryan's book from those I've read in the past is her ability to provide advice by bringing the reader inside important and very emotional human stories. As I read her work, I found myself stopping, needing to consider how a particular story Shannon was sharing connected very directly to financial decisions Patty and I have made and will be making in the future. I feel truly blessed that Shannon is our financial advisor, friend, and confidant.

Sitting across from her in our quarterly meetings always makes us feel—and I'm not embarrassed to say it—cared about and protected. She always is able to help us find the balance between tried-and-true financial principles, along with her constant affirmation that we should always enjoy our money. She constantly reminds us that she is here to keep our financial ship on a proper course. We completely trust Shannon's financial acumen, professional competence, and personal character to provide us with the support that will allow us to enjoy our senior years and guarantee that our estate will benefit our chosen charities and provide our children with more than we might have ever expected. Even with the ups and downs that are an ongoing part of the financial landscape, we leave our meetings with Shannon smiling, knowing we are represented by an advisor we believe in who means so much more to us than our financial portfolio. While it might not be possible for you, the reader, to experience the one-on-one relationship that we have with the author, these pages are beautifully organized, and the writing is clear, engaging, and much more than simply boilerplate. I am sure you will enjoy this read and benefit from Shannon's experiences as a wealth manager.

—**Tom Sullivan,** singer, actor, writer, and motivational speaker

Preface

One of my earliest memories of money is standing in a fast-food restaurant in Laguna Beach. It was summertime, and I was doing a Junior LifeGuards program on Main Beach. At 12:00 p.m., it had been a strenuous day filled with running on the sand and swimming drills in the ocean. That scorching day, my mom joined me for lunch and took me to a local burger stand. I was sandy, hot, and starving. I remember looking for the lowest-cost items to fill me up. Once I had decided, I ran it by my mom to ensure I could order the items I wanted. I essentially asked her, "Can we afford my order?" The young man behind the register told my mom I was so polite to ask. I remember thinking, *I am not being polite; I am terrified of running out of money, being homeless, and not having money for clothes or programs like Junior LifeGuards.* My parents had just gone through a lengthy divorce battle, and money had been used as a weapon. My mom let my sisters and me know daily how little our father was giving us and that we might have to go without. My father told us he was giving so much to my mom that he was going to have to file for bankruptcy. I learned early on that money is capable not only of invoking fear and confusion but also inspiring conflicting narratives. Even a simple hamburger order could potentially be fraught with emotion. Money was complicated and terrifying.

Divorce can leave many financial wounds. At thirteen, I asked to live with my father after my mom moved to another state. It was a really difficult decision, as I had two sisters who moved with my mom, but at the time I felt strongly that I wanted to be in California, where I had grown up. I stayed with my father through high school, and those years had a profound impact on my choice to go into financial services.

My father remarried and divorced again when I was in high school. He complained about the high cost of divorce and the lack of money, just as he had when he and my mom split. At the time, I was a bit numb to the conversation, but I also was beginning to believe this is just what happened when relationships ended in divorce. Again, I saw that money could be used as a weapon. My father did not like his wives to work; he was a surgeon and wanted to earn an income and provide for his family. But in my home, that had come with a cost—power. In private, he criticized his second wife for not being educated enough and not being able to earn a living wage. He called her "uneducated," "lazy," and a "gold digger" in my presence, although he had actively sought out a woman who would not work and would have dinner on the table every night. Having these types of conversations with your high school daughter is not healthy—which seems obvious now, but it was the early '80s and a very different world.

After he divorced his second wife, it was just me and Dad. We had deep conversations over dinner, and he often loved to pick topics for our discussions. Most often, it was his "Money Smarts" lessons. He wanted me to understand money and how it worked in the world. The repeated lesson was about the difference between EQ (emotional quotient) and IQ (intelligence quotient). He fondly reminded me that intelligence was necessary, but our emotional responses to money were more important. I knew he wanted me to be smart, but he was most proud of me when I was emotionally intelligent. To him, this meant I was self-aware, self-regulated, informed, and motivated (I recognize now how ironic his lessons in EQ were, given his own struggles around money and power).

The Money Smarts lessons lasted for years and built a foundation for my lifelong fascination with why people do what they do with their money. But even despite these early financial literacy lessons, my brilliant father had created deep wounds within me through my early experiences of how he treated money during his divorces.

Dad pushed me to start earning money early, at sixteen, encouraging me to be "independent." He never wanted me to be financially vulnerable without the ability to earn an income (again, ironic). When I was a senior in college, he stopped by Barwinkles, the bar where I worked, to say hi and have a drink. Barwinkles was packed that night; the music was loud, and he found a spot at the bar. As the night went on, he became visibly upset as he watched me work. When I asked him what was wrong, he started to tear up, which was rare for my six-foot-five stoic father. He said, "You are studying all day and working at night. I should have helped you more financially. I could have, but I wanted to push you and make you strong." He told me how proud he was of me and how he respected me deeply. I will never forget that moment.

I had earned his respect by working and earning, yet my financial wounds deepened.

I had a profound awareness of my early money wounds, and I shared them with my husband, Chris, when we were engaged. I told him I would always work, keeping my earning potential. As I write this book, we have been married for thirty-four years and have two young adult children. I have always worked full time and strived to be a loving, present wife and mother. It has been challenging to juggle all these roles. But my fear of financial vulnerability from childhood has been a driver all my life. Chris has always understood and supported my professional drive. Over the years, I have learned that I could lean on Chris financially without losing his respect. Today, my professional drive comes from a deep love of what I do, not fear.

My father remains one of the most influential people in my life. He was my rock, one of my greatest fans, and I love him more than I could ever express. Although he created some of my deepest money wounds, he also taught me the importance of EQ versus IQ, ultimately leading me to the behavioral side of money. It brought me to my knees when he died at sixty-two years old from a rare form of Parkinson's that was caused by head trauma he suffered in his early twenties. We had many of our conversations during his illness. One of his final gifts to me was transparency about his own money wounds regarding his deepest fears about money, love, validation, shame, and acceptance. Those discussions created clarity for me in understanding his desire to control money and the wounds he inherited from his parents.

It was his final class in Money Smarts.

Following the Yellow Brick Road

Money usually represents so much more than dollars and cents. It is tied up with our deepest emotional needs: love, power, security, independence, control, and self-worth.

—Olivia Mellan

One of my favorite movies growing up was *The Wizard of Oz*. What intrigued me about the movie was the notion that a regular man behind a curtain could be considered "The Great and Powerful Oz." It only took a small dog, Toto, to pull back the curtain and expose him as just a man. This Great Oz convinced everyone in Emerald City that he alone had power over them. All they needed was to gain his favor in order to have their wishes granted. When the Great Oz was exposed as a fraud, Dorothy, Scarecrow, Lion, and the Tin Man learned that they carried their gifts within themselves. In the end, they could find their way home using what had been there all along.

When it comes to money, many of us are seeking the Great and Powerful Oz! We are searching for the easy way, a way to never have to worry about money again—a way to solve our problems without ever having to look inside ourselves. We scour the internet and watch videos on how to invest, how to get rich, or how to win the lottery. We idolize and envy those with money, often without examining the quality of their lives.

In my many years of working with people and their money, I have felt like Toto pulling back the curtain to expose the truth: We all carry deep-seated beliefs about money that most of us do not recognize or want to discuss. I've actually given a name to this phenomenon that holds people back from having satisfying financial lives—I call it "scar tissue." This scar tissue is a residual memory, often left by a wounding experience with money based on fear, shame, disappointments, cultural expectations, and habits. In my experience, what is holding most of us back financially is not the lack of the next hot stock tip, job promotion, or an unexpected windfall. What truly impacts most people's financial success is their own personal behaviors, beliefs, and habits around money.

My favorite line from *The Wizard of Oz* is spoken by Glinda the Good Witch. She tells Dorothy near the end of the film, "You've always had the power, my dear; you just had to learn it for yourself." I wrote this book because I, too, believe we can all find our way home to financial enjoyment.

My Why Behind This Book

As much as I have loved my chosen career as a wealth manager in financial services, our industry has missed the mark on how we help people with their money. We do a disservice to our clients when we focus on investment returns and stock market ticker tapes running across the front of a news program. We use confusing terminology and overcomplicate money management. We have created an industry many people do not trust and feel intimidated to approach to get help unless they have significant assets. While many advisors are creating practices based on planning and alignment of money with clients' values rather than just stock picking, it is my firm belief that we need to continue to evolve toward a gold standard of always considering the human side of money.

For the last three decades, I have had a front-row seat to the financial lives of hundreds of individuals and families. What I have learned is that money is emotional—always. Many believe we can separate our emotions and money; I have often heard, "I am not emotional about money and can make 100 percent logical decisions." After all these years, I cannot recall any human who did not have some money scar tissue.

In our bodies, scar tissue is what remains after a wound has healed. The same is true of financial wounds. What are financial wounds? They come in many forms. For you, they may be memories of your parents arguing over bills, your experience of losing a job, getting divorced, experiencing bankruptcy, living through a recession, going hungry, or being told, "Sorry, we don't have enough money." These invisible wounds, whether you acknowledge them or not, come to define your money thoughts, creating the behavioral patterns that keep you from attaining your goals. Real work toward financial happiness can only occur when your money wounds and their resulting behaviors are addressed in financial planning.

Financial behavior patterns describe what we do with our

money on an unconscious level. They explain, from an emotional perspective, why and how we make financial decisions. Traditional finance assumes that we are always rational and seek to maximize our wealth at every opportunity. However, behavioral finance recognizes that we may often act irrationally as the result of psychological biases, emotions, and cognitive errors.

With that reality in mind, I wrote this book to profoundly change your thoughts and actions around money. I know it can be done—no matter how deep or hidden your financial wounds are—because for decades, clients have come into my office with the weight of their financial lives keeping them awake at night, their minds ruminating on money worries. I have developed a process that helps them align their money with their values to create a financial plan and find a new way to think about their money.

In the following pages, I will teach you how to manage money in alignment with your goals and create a solid financial foundation for yourself and your loved ones. I will do this with a two-pronged approach: 1) by helping you identify your unconscious and behavioral biases around money; and 2) by giving you practical ways to create a financial life that aligns with your values, using the tenets of both behavioral *and* traditional finance. I will also share with you why financial confidence is so elusive for most people. Spoiler alert: The answer is rarely the need for more money.

Monetary success is ultimately about how we react to financial challenges and interact with the resources we have. Let's start by digging into your financial mind.

PART I

The Basics of Behavioral Finance

CHAPTER 1

What Are Money Wounds and Why Do They Matter?

Never underestimate the power of anyone's story . . .

—Abigail Johnson

Money wounds can inspire us to take actions and even develop habits about money. These invisible wounds can come to define our thoughts about money and encourage patterns of behavior that keep us from attaining our goals, achieving financial satisfaction, and being happy. Financial wounds leave financial scar tissue because so often these wounds occur in childhood or earlier in life and endure within us as unexamined pain points that influence our behavior around money long after the precipitating incidents are forgotten.

You might find it unexpectedly challenging to talk about or identify your financial wounds. In our society, discussions around money are still considered impolite, making it difficult to examine our own experiences and internally held beliefs about money. As a financial advisor, one of the essential questions I have learned to ask is, "What have you inherited financially?" When I ask this, I am not looking for a dollar amount. Instead, I am asking my client to identify the emotions and ideas about money they learned from their family, friends, and community that continue to influence them as adults. I have found that naming and unpacking these often-painful experiences can help us to achieve the financial happiness many of us so desperately seek.

Money Wounds: Expectations, Regret, Fear, Shame, and Power and Control

Money wounds typically manifest in my clients through their association of money with certain persistent negative feelings or influences. While you may experience different feelings when you reflect on the way your own financial scar tissue impacts your current relationship with money, I share the case studies that follow to illustrate the kinds of powerful, negative feelings my clients often uncover and work through while examining their own money wounds.

EXPECTATIONS

Society—our families, peers, and social media—often tells us that success is defined by specific financial accomplishments. Therefore, living up to external expectations of how to handle our money can make us feel like we are doing "the right thing," regardless of whether or not we achieve our own desires.

When I first met with Allison and John, they told me what they most desired was travel, but they had just purchased a home.

After covering the new monthly mortgage payment, insurance, and taxes, they had very little money left. I asked them why they'd bought the house instead of pursuing their dream of traveling. They told me they thought it was the next step for them. It was *the right thing to do.*

As we continued to talk, it became apparent to me that their parents had pressured them to buy a home and extend themselves to do it. Their parents had good intentions, but Allison and John were working professionals in their early thirties, recently married, and without kids. They pictured themselves on vacations to exotic destinations, but the home purchase had demolished their cash reserves.

Allison and John weren't even consciously aware of the external pressure that had driven them to buy the house. They had been raised to believe that owning a home—the bigger, the better—should be their top priority. They believed that the purchase had been their idea. They were "house poor," stuck in their jobs, miserable, and mystified as to how owning the home of their dreams had made them so unhappy and unfulfilled.

The room fell silent when I told them to consider selling the house. My clients' overwhelming sense of responsibility to do what made them look successful to the outside world was stealing their happiness. And while at first Allison and John were stunned, eventually their excitement started to grow. Finally, I could hear it in their voices as they talked about living on their own terms with their own priorities.

The good news for Allison and John was that home prices had continued to go up, and they had built up a little bit of equity. It was pretty easy for them to sell the home, and they found a smaller one that fit within their budget. Between the money earned from the sale of their home and the new, lower mortgage payment, they could keep their commitment to saving for retirement while starting to travel. Not staying trapped by the external expectations of their family changed their lives.

Reflection

- What external expectations are driving your financial decisions or frustrations?
- What internal expectations do you have of yourself around money?
- Do you feel like you are "free" to make money choices that align with your desires?

REGRET

Regret, as defined by the *Oxford Dictionary*, is "a feeling of sadness, repentance, or disappointment over something that has happened, been done, or not done."[1] Allianz Life's 2024 Annual Retirement Study revealed that 55 percent of Generation X individuals wish they had saved more for retirement. This study also noted that only 62 percent of Gen Xers feel confident about their financial future, compared to 82 percent of baby boomers and 77 percent of millennials.[2]

Regret is a powerful emotion. Often it will keep us from seeking professional help until we get our financial house in order. The pain of regret can be so powerful that we would rather live with it than tell another human about our mistakes and ask for help. The key findings of the Allianz study cited are the same things I hear in my office when I meet with new clients. They will often start off the conversation using the language of regret: "I should have started saving sooner," "We spend too much money," or "I know I don't know much about investing." Often they have delayed seeking help with their financial goals for years because of a combination of the scar tissue of regret and their own judgment of themselves.

Regret also shows up in how we spend our money on things that do not "buy" us happiness. For me, it was a Pontiac Bonneville. Bonnevilles were in production for almost half a century, ending in 2005. If you own a classic Bonneville, I hope you love it. But for me, that car represented a financial decision I regretted. My big, green four-door Bonneville was the first car I bought myself. My husband and I were living in Washington, DC, at the time, and I was driving the used Bronco my father had given me for college. I loved that car, but I'd put so many miles on it that it was time for a change. I was excited to buy myself a car, and I was ready. I knew what I could afford. My husband and I were both new in our careers, and there was no way I could pay cash, so I figured out how much of a payment I could handle, decided on a target price, and started looking at used cars.

I needed something old enough to be inexpensive but new enough to take me through the next few years. Additionally, I wanted a car that was not too flashy, one that had reasonable repair costs. I tried to be practical, but I was busy and needed a vehicle right away, so—as I often did in my twenties—I rushed the decision.

I tried to convince myself of how much I loved my new car, but every time I got into the Bonneville, it didn't feel like "me." I didn't understand what I'd done until I met a good friend for a business lunch. As we got out of our cars in the parking lot, he said, "You know, Shannon, I would never have pictured you driving a green Bonneville! Was that your dad's car?"

At that moment, it clicked: I'd bought the Bonneville because I thought my dad would approve. He would think it was practical and would be pleased that it was a good value with a price that was lower than what I could afford. It sounded reasonable . . . except I'd compromised. Instead of doing what *I* wanted, I'd done what I thought I *should* do. Of course, we do this all the time—but where are all these *shoulds* coming from?

As it turned out, mine came from my father. He'd always been clear that a car was a depreciating asset, more of a utility than something to be enjoyed. The irony is that later in life, he drove a luxury car that *he* wanted! As he got older, he overcame his own family beliefs that purchases should be practical without exception.

Looking back now at buying that green Bonneville, I can see the two mistakes I made that had led me to the wrong decision. The first was that I was in a rush. By not slowing down to think through a decision, I cost myself more money—and that cost me enjoyment. My second mistake was giving in to the set of *shoulds* I had learned from my father without considering whether or not they applied to my current situation.

These days, I typically pay cash for my cars and keep them for at least ten years. I only kept the Bonneville for three. I regretted my decision every time I got into the car, and as soon as I was making more money, I bought a new car. I took more time and saved up more money so I could pay cash for the car I loved. I kept that car for eleven years and loved it until the day I let it go.

How often do we do this? Many people aren't happy with their lives even when they have enough income to live the lifestyle they desire. We let our unexamined beliefs drive our purchases: "I'm not worthy of that car that I really want" or "I can't afford it." But are those beliefs true? We'll never know until we've actually run the numbers. If we only rely on the *shoulds*, we use our resources to buy things that don't make us happy—and then we live with the regret that we don't have what we want when we had the money to buy it.

Reflection

- Do you have financial regret?
- What reasoning did you have for making the decisions you regret?
- What unexamined *shoulds* can you identify behind these decisions?

FEAR

I do not currently have any tattoos, but if I were to get one, I would put *Noli Timere* on my arm; it is Latin for "Do Not Be Afraid." Fear is wrapped up with the loss of control, and I witness it crippling people daily. Unfortunately, fear is often present in our relationship with money, and it keeps people from the lives they want to live. Embracing fear can bleed over into worries over the potential loss of a job or the inability to meet a financial emergency. Projected over a lifetime, the wounds caused by fear can keep you up at night worrying about your investments going to zero, having to support a family member, looming debt, not being able to retire or send our kids to college, or even homelessness.

As we've discussed, our financial wounds and subsequent scar tissue are often inherited from our families. In essence, these beliefs may be ancestral, heritable, and certainly intergenerational. Research indicates that financial trauma affects a substantial portion of the US population. For instance, studies have shown that generational financial trauma, which can be passed down through family lines, affects many individuals and leads to negative financial behaviors such as avoidance, overspending, or being overly frugal. These behaviors often arise from deeply ingrained emotional responses to past financial hardships experienced by previous generations.[3]

For example, if your grandparents grew up during the Great Depression, they may instill saving money and not spending on lavish items into your family values. More recently, with the stock and housing declines in the Great Recession, we are seeing millennials coming of age during 2007–2009 with a greater aversion to risk than older generations; they are quicker to jump out of stock investments and focus on long-term money. Do you think the fear they must have witnessed with the 57 percent decline in the S&P 500 during those years had an impact on their investing style? Millennials were more likely than any other generation to flee the stock market during last year's rout, which meant they were also more likely to miss out on the subsequent rally.[4] Fear is a powerful wound.

Fear and Scams

We have seen a significant increase in scammers in the last few years, especially with electronic access to our money. Fear significantly contributes to fraud by making us more vulnerable to manipulation. Fraudsters often exploit fear to push people into making irrational decisions or taking actions they would otherwise avoid. This fear has a calculable cost: A 2023 AARP study determined that Americans over sixty lose $28.3 billion each year to fraud.[5] The Federal Trade Commission, seeking to account for unreported losses, estimated fraudsters stole a staggering $137 billion in 2022, including $48 billion from older adults.[6]

Recently, I was visiting one of my closest friends for the night, and we settled in together to watch *The Beekeeper*, a movie released in 2024 (movie spoilers ahead). The opening scene was one I knew too well: A retiree is sitting at her computer, and a pop-up appears on her screen indicating she has a virus in her computer, but if she clicks the button, an agent will help her resolve the issue. She clicks on the button, and the scene then goes to a room of scammers now watching her through her computer, taking her through her passwords for her financial accounts. Within moments, her life savings are gone. She is devastated. That's when I started pacing the room. I had no idea what this movie was about, and it was far too realistic for me. Everything happened at movie speed, squeezed into two hours, but the elements are ones that I see far too often.

You may believe you will always be able to spot a scam. Still, they are becoming very sophisticated, and I have had some highly educated clients and friends almost give their life savings away to highly technology-based and compelling schemes. Fear is the base emotion that allows these scammers to convince people to give them their hard-earned money.

FEAR-BASED EMOTIONS SCAMMERS EVOKE TO GET YOU TO GIVE UP YOUR MONEY

1. **Urgency and Panic:** Scammers often create a sense of urgency, invoking fear that something bad will happen unless

immediate action is taken. For example, people might receive calls about "urgent" issues like tax penalties, bank account freezes, or legal action unless they provide sensitive information or payment.

2. **Fear of Missing Out (FOMO):** In investment frauds, fear of missing out on a lucrative opportunity can cause victims to bypass due diligence.

3. **Fear of Authority Figures:** Scammers impersonate authority figures such as government agents, police officers, or financial institution representatives, leveraging the fear of legal consequences or financial loss. This fear makes victims more compliant.

4. **Fear of Embarrassment:** Fraudsters may blackmail victims by threatening to expose personal information, photos, or other compromising details. The fear of social or reputational damage makes the victim more likely to comply.

5. **Fear of Judgment:** In romance or relationship fraud, victims may be too embarrassed to admit they've been duped, allowing the fraud to continue longer and the perpetrator to extract more money or personal information.

6. **Fear of Financial Instability:** Many fraud schemes, like Ponzi schemes or investment scams, prey on people's fear of economic uncertainty or their desperation for financial security. Fraudsters promise guaranteed returns, playing on the fear of losing financial stability.

7. **Fear of Financial Consequences:** Scammers may threaten severe consequences for unpaid debt, such as arrest or lawsuits, pushing victims to make payments or divulge personal financial information out of fear.

8. **Fear for Physical Health:** Fraudsters exploit fears surrounding health by promoting fake cures or miracle treatments, especially during health crises (e.g., pandemics). Victims, motivated by the fear of illness or death, may pay large sums for useless or harmful products.

9. **Safety of Loved Ones:** Scammers may call with false claims that a loved one is in danger (e.g., kidnapping scams) and demand a ransom. The fear for the safety of a family member or friend compels quick, unthought-out reactions.

Reflection

- What money fears do you think you may have?
- How did you develop these fears?
- In what way do you think these fears affect your relationship with money?

SHAME

Shame is the strongest emotion I see around money. We make a mistake and feel we should have known better. The embarrassment about this can keep us from seeking an expert to help heal the wounds shame causes. Shame drives secrecy, loneliness, and pain.

Mike and Judy are good friends of our family. One evening when we were together at a function, the topic of money and what was important to them came up. The conversation was casual, but I could tell there was something more, and when they called the next day to make an appointment, it became apparent some part of our discussion had hit a nerve.

Mike and Judy arrived at my office. Mike said, "Shannon, we need to talk to you. I know we are friends, but how you talk about money and ask questions is unlike anyone we have worked with." He started to quietly tell me the story of an investment professional with whom he had placed money. He had entrusted not only a significant amount of his family money to this person, but he had also influenced several philanthropic groups he worked with and loved to invest with the same man. Judy held Mike's hand, gently encouraging him as he spoke. They both cried, and I wept with them as he recounted the story. Unfortunately, the "investment professional" was a fraud, and he disappeared with the money that had been invested. The shame had broken Mike. He felt like he had let down his family and the nonprofit community he was tightly aligned with. They had been working for years to bring this man to justice and restore Mike's good name. I was grateful they were in my office and had trusted me with their pain.

Once I fully understood the situation, I asked them, "What do you want to happen from here financially?" It was a hard question, as they'd never imagined being in the position of rebuilding their retirement again from scratch this late in life. We rolled up our sleeves with a lot of trust and love, then went to work. Mike and Judy agreed to be honest, candid, and transparent with me through the process.

Their recovery took years, and they continued working in their professions longer than either of them had anticipated, but some wonderful things happened along the way, too. Today, they are retired with enough money to enjoy their lives. I still get tears in my eyes when I reflect on the pain they endured at the hands of a financial scammer and the years they suffered with the weight of their mistake. Admitting their shame gave them the freedom to start over.

Shame can also be cultural. Luci and George had immigrated to the United States. They were not college educated and were very proud of their seventeen-year-old daughter, Sabrina, a great student who already had college acceptance letters and scholarships. They were crushed when Sabrina told them that she was pregnant at seventeen. The family was sure she would be trapped in the same poverty they had worked so hard to escape.

When I spoke with Sabrina, she told me that she would marry the baby's father but still wanted to go to college. But she was starting to have doubts. Her parents' negativity about her future made her question whether she was still "worth" the investment of the scholarship she had been awarded. Sabrina could have allowed her shame to paralyze her. Instead, she agreed to work with me on a plan.

I had known Sabrina since she was nine, and she trusted my guidance. She promised to talk with me twice yearly and follow my financial recommendations. As a result, Sabrina had her baby girl, graduated from college, and landed a six-figure job. She and her husband now own a home, have no credit card debt, and have a healthy cash reserve. It was not easy, but they have created a solid financial foundation, remained married, and are now expecting their third child.

There are tens of thousands of people in the world who have allowed the shame surrounding a youthful mistake to define their financial lives forever. Sometimes you need an outside voice to help you sort out your wounds and the shame you've absorbed from other people. With this support, you can trust yourself and remember that you are worth it.

> ### Reflection
>
> - Have you made a mistake in the past that makes you feel you are unworthy of financial success now?
>
> - Do you have a financial situation you are unwilling to discuss or are you making excuses for a financial struggle to protect your self-esteem?
>
> - Can you identify any financial difficulties that seem insurmountable? Are you hopeless or despairing, feeling like you will never escape the situation?

POWER AND CONTROL

Those who have money are often more highly regarded in our world. We read their books and watch TV shows and movies about how they made their wealth. The lottery is as popular as ever! Why? Because we feel that if we had more money, we would have more choices, freedom, and power. We imagine that with money, life is more manageable, without worry, and happier. As I mentioned during the story of my parents' divorce, money can become the marker in an ongoing power struggle within a family or relationship. If this was the model you saw growing up, it might also be the backdrop of your current life. What was modeled financially for you growing up?

Money power is not always negative, but if I asked you if you would prefer to control the money in your life or be controlled *by* money, what would you choose? It's not unusual for one person in a household to control how money is spent. This system can work if it's by mutual agreement. However, the situation becomes toxic when the person in control limits access to accounts, withholds money, makes big purchases or investments without consulting the other partner, or otherwise weaponizes household finances to manipulate the personal relationship.

Establishing communication about money requires a larger conversation about the nature of your relationship itself rather than simply allowing yourself to fall into traditional roles. A stay-at-home spouse in a caregiving role for children or aging parents can feel "trapped" due to their lack of financial independence. Most of us know someone who has stayed married because they couldn't afford to leave. If the relationship is unhealthy, the income earner can use that leverage to keep the relationship using the power of money, even if the relationship is abusive. In the extreme, this dynamic can result in forged signatures, lies about the household's financial health, or even physical abuse. Don't accept a potentially dangerous financial situation simply because "that's how Mom and Dad did it."

Hannah and Clay found me in a magazine article. They had just moved to Southern California for a job. They were finding the real estate market very expensive and were looking for a financial advisor to help them decide on how much they should invest in a house alongside their other goals. Hannah was initially nervous, not about speaking with a financial advisor, but about money in general. She appeared to be in a negative spiral when we met. She was sure they had made a bad decision moving into such a high cost-of-living area. She had clearly been ruminating on calculations in her mind, and she appeared to have been getting very little sleep.

When I asked them why they'd reached out to me and what I could do to help them, Hannah quickly started by saying, "I think we have made a horrible mistake. We cannot afford any of the homes in the area we want to live in. And if we do buy a home, we will be house poor, and we will never be able to do anything fun. Our adult kids live in the area. We thought it would be a good idea, but now we realize this move will bankrupt us." She barely drew a breath as she spoke. Her worry and deep pain were clear.

After Hannah had finished, Clay spoke in a much calmer tone. "We have a high income, have saved a considerable amount of money, and I think we will be okay." Clay went on to say they would like to build a plan around their new cost of living and continue to save for their retirement, which was about ten years out. He indicated that they loved to travel and spend time spoiling their grandkids.

The disparate tone of Hannah and Clay's thoughts about money was clear. But it was also clear that Hannah's negative rumination around money was not new. In fact, Clay was very calm as Hannah expressed some of the apparent panic she was experiencing about the cost of their decision to move. When they outlined their financial position for me, their priority was determining what they could comfortably spend on a home, taking their other personal goals into consideration. They had done a great job saving, had no debt, made enough from the sale of their previous home for a sizable down payment, and were well on their way to retirement savings. But Hannah commented throughout the discussion about "running out of money" and being "house poor." She was authentically concerned—one might even say *distraught*. The couple joked about her being a "worrier" when it came to money and being "frugal."

I have enjoyed working with Hannah and Clay over the years; Hannah remains worried about money, even now as they have enough to retire. In a recent meeting, she joined the Zoom meeting before Clay did. Clay was thinking about leaving his job, and Hannah was panicked. This opportunity allowed me to ask her why she was still so worried when I had clearly demonstrated they were financially independent enough to retire. Even if Clay did leave his job, financially they could still meet all their goals, including retirement.

As it turned out, Hannah was no stranger to financial scar tissue. She shared with me that her first husband had used money as power and given her an "allowance," but it was never enough to buy groceries for the family. If she spent more, he would rage at her. Although it had been decades since Hannah had left that marriage, the pain of money scarcity that her first husband had created still left her anxious around money.

While she was able to recognize where her money anxiety came from, the panic around not having enough or running out was still a deep-seated wound. By the time Hannah had finished telling me her story, Clay had joined our conversation and added with a warm laugh, "We will have to continue to remind her, Shannon, that she is okay financially. The abuse she endured has left what you call 'deep financial wounds.'"

Further Reflections

- Have you suffered financial wounds?

- What is your financial inheritance? Take a moment and reflect on your financial history.

- Who taught you about money?

- What experiences have shaped your habits around how you feel, interact, and react to money?

- What is important to you about money? What is the purpose of money in your life?

Money Smarts

- Money wounds are negative experiences or memories we have around money that impact our current relationship with it.

- The most common causes of financial scar tissue (lingering memories or habits from wounds) are expectations, regret, fear, shame, and power and control.

CHAPTER 2

Behavioral Finance
versus
Traditional Finance

Personal finance is more personal
than it is finance.

—Tim Maurer

W e all feel the legitimate, scientifically proven impact of behavioral finance. However, our current financial system approaches money traditionally. Traditional finance assumes that all investors are rational and make the best decisions based on the objective information available to them. I often hear people say they need to be "more knowledgeable in the area of investing" and "should have focused more on it" earlier in their lives. The assumption is that if they knew more about investing, they could be more successful or happier with their financial decisions. This is a traditional approach.

Behavioral Finance

Amassing knowledge about finance and investing may have felt difficult in the past, but today, with our ability to google any topic and watch videos on YouTube or TEDx Talks, information has been greatly democratized. However, recent statistics show that despite this fact, worldwide only one in three adults is financially literate; only 33 percent of adults worldwide are financially literate. This means that around 3.5 billion adults—granted most of them in Global South economies—lack an understanding of basic financial concepts.[1]

We need to ask why, especially in developed countries, the financial literacy numbers look so low. It is my experience that just seeking a higher level of money knowledge is not enough; we need to consider the behavioral side of money to increase literacy. In the first chapter, I wrote about financial experiences that wounded us, leaving "scar tissue" in our psyches. Recognizing that you've had these experiences is a great starting point in your financial journey. These experiences inevitably shape our behaviors around money, both positively and negatively. Each of us has our unique mix of emotions, blind spots, and influences that can radically change our outcomes with money. Our behaviors can manifest in many ways, and this is one of the critical reasons even traditionally financially literate investors often never find financial satisfaction.

> Each of us has our unique mix of emotions, blind spots, and influences that can radically change our outcomes with money.

There are books filled with psychological terms we can use to describe what drives our relationship with money. Understand there is no shame if much of this information is new or if intimidation has hindered your ability to ask questions. Your current degree of financial literacy is not a reflection on your intelligence, success, or potential for financial satisfaction. In fact, research shows "there is no evidence that income is associated with financial literacy."[2] This means you can be a high-income earner or have significant assets and still not be financially literate. If you struggle with financial literacy, you're in good company.

Financial literacy acts as a bridge between understanding unconscious money beliefs (money scripts), correcting irrational financial decisions (behavioral biases), and addressing harmful financial patterns (dysfunction). By increasing financial literacy, individuals can gain the insight and skills necessary to break free from negative financial cycles shaped by past experiences.

The connection between financial literacy and the three areas in behavioral finance—money scripts, behavioral biases, and dysfunction—can be significant, especially considering how past experiences and wounds shape financial behaviors.

Money Scripts

The unconscious beliefs each of us has developed concerning money and life are called money scripts. Money scripts are most often formed in childhood, shaped by both direct and indirect messages we receive about money from our parents. While many may know something is amiss, no one has described it better, in my opinion, than Brad Klontz, a leader in understanding mental health and money approaches: "Addressing the past can be a critical component of achieving financial health, especially for clients with long-term patterns of problematic money behavior."[3]

What is the difference between money scripts and money wounds? Money scripts are unconscious beliefs or attitudes about money that individuals develop, often during childhood. These scripts are usually learned from parents, caregivers, or cultural influences. Money wounds are emotional or psychological traumas related to money that result from negative financial experiences. These wounds can be caused by events such as financial hardship, bankruptcy, parental financial struggles, or being shamed about money. They are closely related, and often a script is created out of a wound.

If money scripts are left unchallenged, we can develop self-destructive and self-limiting habits with our money. Below is a list of money scripts that Klontz identifies in his book *Facilitating Financial Health*.[4]

Money Scripts: Do you see any that may be limiting your financial happiness?

1. More money will make things better.
2. Money is bad.
3. I don't deserve money.
4. I deserve to spend money.
5. There will never be enough money.
6. There will always be enough money.
7. Money is unimportant.
8. Money will give me meaning.
9. It is not nice (or necessary) to talk about money.
10. If you are good, the universe will supply all your needs.

Identifying and challenging a money script you have developed is possible, but it will take work. Without your conscious knowledge, these money scripts can be lying at the root of your habits and how you respond to money.

One of my clients, Tara, loves to play tennis and plays several days a week. Tennis is an active sport and can be hard on our bodies, especially as we age. Her money script is, "There will never be enough money, and I could lose it all tomorrow." While we may not be privy to why Tara has this particular money script, it is imperative that she begins to investigate and understand it. Maybe this was an idea her parents raised her with. No matter its origin, Tara is aware of her money script. Still, meeting after meeting, year after year, I have to remind her that she has enough money to buy proper tennis shoes so she does not risk injury. She has more money than I anticipate she will need through retirement, but she cannot bring herself to spend out of fear. Tara is

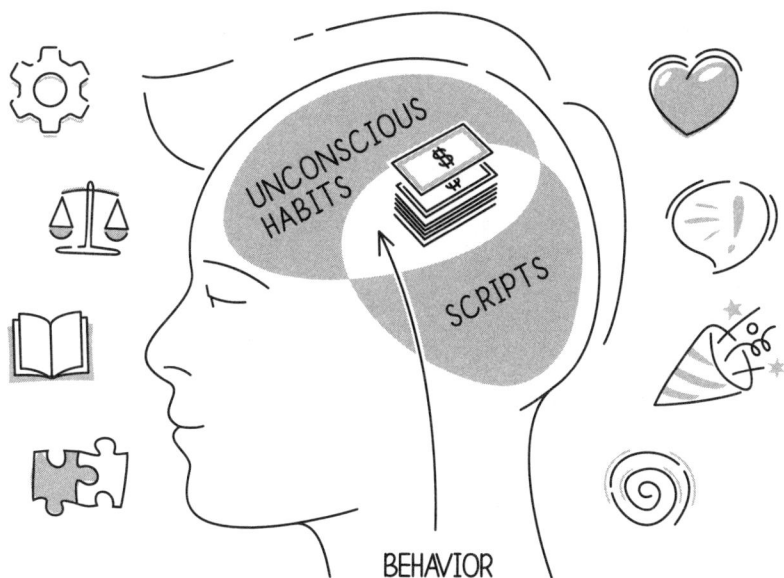

extremely frugal and bright. She and I always laugh when she "asks for permission" to spend her money on items that others with her wealth wouldn't think twice about. She knows it is a money script, but it's deeply entrenched. These scripts become a part of our scar tissue. And many of us will need to return to the root of our scripts as a reminder to stay healthy when it comes to how we speak to themselves and others about money.

Recently, I had a client who had just inherited a significant amount of life insurance money after his father's death. He was single, in his early thirties, and had been teaching for a few years. He told me that money was not important to him. When I asked him if he wanted to just donate the money, he was clear that he needed it for a home and living expenses, as his teacher's income was not enough to support a purchase of a home in the area he lived. I asked him why he felt the money was something he didn't consider important. He shared with me that he always felt his father was disappointed he didn't go into a career that paid a more significant income. He had developed a disdain for money. He wanted his father to be proud of his love of teaching without commentary on the income potential. Now that his father was gone, the money represented that judgment and still held a sting. We created a plan for him to not only purchase a home but also, over time, use some of the money for his passion, which was education. He eventually developed a scholarship fund for new teachers. In working with his old money script, we had created a positive purpose for his inheritance that brought him money satisfaction.

Reflection

- How was money talked about in your household growing up? Was it a source of stress, joy, secrecy, or conflict?
- If you could describe your relationship with money in one sentence, what would it be?
- What money habits or beliefs would you like to pass on to others, such as your children or mentees?

Money Biases

Your brain makes more than thirty-five thousand decisions each day, according to Eva Krockow, lecturer at the University of Leicester in the United Kingdom.[5] By the evening, you may be exhausted, but you can't quite understand why. Our brains make many of these decisions really quickly, so we would be unable to slow down the pace and carefully analyze everything we've decided in a day. We've developed a way to make these decisions that often becomes a habitual response. Psychology calls these heuristics, a way our brains develop shortcuts to quickly make decisions—often known as mental shortcuts. When it comes to money, we create biases that help us make financial decisions, and these are often based on our past money experiences.

By identifying your own experiences around money, you can evaluate or recognize the biases you have developed to aid you in making money decisions. Once you've identified them, you can reevaluate your beliefs and habits to determine if they align with your financial goals and desires. There are many types of bias, but here are some of the most common:

- **Loss Aversion:** The desire to avoid loss for any reason. Losses are felt far more severely than any gains.

- **Anchoring Bias:** The tendency to give more weight to the first piece of information we receive in decision-making.

- **Herd Instinct:** The decision to follow others and imitate group behaviors rather than decide independently based on our own research or desires.

- **Overconfidence Bias:** Thinking we are better in some areas than we really are.

- **Confirmation Bias:** The tendency to search for, interpret, favor, and recall information in a way that confirms or supports a belief we already have.

Family, friends, and those who influence us can hugely impact our money decisions and our bias. They usually have great intentions but do not know our whole financial picture. The same is true for the information we find online and on social media. As I am writing this book, we are seeing this play out in a very negative way in the cryptocurrency arena. Cryptocurrency companies have even used celebrities to influence millions of people to purchase this high-risk, currently unregulated investment. It is up to the individual to research why a celebrity or other well-known person is promoting any product. I err on the side of caution, especially when it comes to anything financial. Please do your research! I wish I could tell everyone, "Buyer beware—endorsements are normally paid, and there is an incredible amount of fine print." I also tend to believe that if something sounds too good to be true financially, it usually is.

Gary and Sue became my clients in the late 1990s. At the time they started working with me, they were both in their late fifties or early sixties and really focused on getting ready for retirement. I researched the cost of living, when they wanted to retire, and the assets that they had invested. Each had a 401(k), IRAs, and non-qualified other money that wasn't retirement- or tax-deferred. I put together a financial plan for them and invested for them over the years of 1997, 1998, and 1999. They got spectacular returns on a balanced portfolio—it was mind-boggling.

In 1999, Gary and I made an appointment to review his and Sue's progress. I remember that day so clearly: Gary and Sue sat across from me as I excitedly shared that they had earned a whopping 38 percent on their balanced portfolio in the last year. Wow! They were in great shape to retire in the next couple of years.

Gary was not impressed—and he was not happy. He explained that when he went out to the mailbox each evening, he would run into his neighbor, and they would talk about their investments. Remember, this was when stocks, especially technology stocks, went wild. So, Gary and his neighbor compared notes, and the neighbor bragged that he had made a 79 percent return on his technology stocks over the last year.

In comparison, Gary was deeply disappointed in his own portfolio. He felt that I had him grossly underweighted in technology even though he had significant exposure that was driving his gains. He wanted me to go all in, 100 percent, on technology stocks.

I understood his frustration, and I commiserated with him. I told him I knew it must be hard to hear that his neighbor made 79 percent when he "only" got 38 percent. I reminded him that he and Sue were only a few years away from retirement and the amount of risk they took was an important consideration. I explained that I was baffled by the technology companies' lack of book value (assets) versus what their stock was worth. I warned him that the technology sector seemed overvalued—the price-to-earnings ratios didn't make any sense—and while I didn't have a crystal ball, it made me nervous.

I wanted to retain Gary and Sue as clients, but I felt very uncomfortable putting more of their money in technology. I advised Gary about the level of risk that he should (and shouldn't) be taking this close to retirement. I tried to get him to understand that a 38 percent return was spectacular in a well-balanced port-folio for 1998, far above what we estimated they needed annually to meet their big goal of retirement. Gary wasn't having it. He was convinced he had missed out and wanted to be 100 percent in technology stock. When I told him I was uncomfortable exe-cuting that for them, he fired me as their advisor, withdrew their money, and took it to another broker.

About seven months later, in 2000, I was offered a position as a field vice president and asked to run an office in another state, and my husband and I moved to Texas. I hadn't spoken with Gary since that day in my office. He had transferred his investments out of my management two weeks after that difficult meeting in 1999.

One afternoon in 2001, I got a call at my Dallas office. My administrative assistant said the call was from Gary in Washington, DC. When I picked up the phone, Gary said, "Hi, Shannon; I have been trying to locate you for some time. I owe you an apol-ogy." They had lost more than 80 percent of the value of their investments. "I realize now how hard you tried to convince me to stay with a balanced portfolio. I have thought about you every day. I just want to thank you for trying."

We had a nice conversation, but I felt sick when I hung up the phone.

The day Gary fired me was one of the hardest days I've had in my career, but it was much harder to learn that he had now lost 80 percent of his life savings. He sold when the markets were down;

he couldn't stand to hang on and wait for recovery. Emotionally it was just too much. He told me that he would probably have to work another ten to fifteen years now and didn't know if he'd ever be able to invest again because of his fear of loss.

Behavioral finance introduces the idea that investors are not always rational and are often influenced by psychological biases and emotions. Cognitive biases like overconfidence, loss aversion, and herd behavior can lead to irrational financial decisions and market anomalies.[6] There were a few money biases at work in Gary and Sue's story. First, Gary anchored (anchoring bias) his neighbor's return as what he should be getting and allowed that to influence his decision-making. He also displayed herd instinct by following his neighbor's decision to be all in on technology stocks, although he and his neighbor may have had different wealth levels and time horizons for their goals. And finally, he had looked for evidence to confirm his belief that technology stock could not lose (confirmation bias). Gary had searched for, interpreted, and favored information that confirmed his beliefs.

Reflection

- Can you think of a time when a financial decision didn't go as planned? What bias might have influenced your choice?

- Have you ever made a financial decision because "everyone else was doing it," without fully understanding the reasons behind it?

- Do you actively seek out information that supports your current financial beliefs or decisions while ignoring opposing views?

Money Disorders

In some people, difficulty with money goes far beyond the normal stress that most of us experience from time to time. These are often referred to as "money disorders" and have various levels. A lack of money rarely causes them but rather often results from emotional difficulties and intense, unresolved emotions. There are various levels of money disorders ranging from mild to severe. Money disorders can and do include full-fledged money addiction that is as real and destructive as an addiction to alcohol or other drugs.[7]

Shame often creates a merry-go-round with addiction that makes it incredibly hard to stop or get off the ride. The authors of *Facilitating Financial Health* list the following as the symptoms of money disorders:[8]

- Anxiety, worry, depression, or resentment about the individual's financial situation
- A lack of savings and investments
- Repeated, failed attempts to change problematic financial behaviors
- The use of money in an attempt to control others
- Excessive debt
- Bankruptcy
- Ongoing conflict with a spouse or others around money
- Compulsive financial behaviors
- Overspending
- Miserliness
- Preoccupation with material things, spending, work, or gambling

- Lying to others about financial behaviors
- Illegal actions meant to support compulsive financial behaviors
- Underearning
- Excessive financial risk-taking

Many of us may find we have bits and pieces of these disorders, so if you see yourself in several, do not panic that you have a *disorder*, as that can be taken as a negative word. If any of these symptoms of disorders are disrupting your financial life, it may be time to take a deeper dive into what may be causing you to interact with your resources in a negative way. If you are experiencing a money disorder, please seek professional help.

Reflection

- Can you identify any financial behaviors that have caused significant distress or problems in your life?
- Have others expressed concern about your financial behaviors or decisions? What was your reaction?
- When was the last time you felt overwhelmed or out of control in managing your finances?

Traditional versus Behavioral Finance

It's often difficult to recognize a money bias, story, or disorder, especially in ourselves, but if you start to listen closely to how people talk about money, you will find clues to the money stories of your friends and family. I have a close group of friends who meet once a month for an appetizer and a drink after work before we head home. We decompress and share about what may have happened since we last saw one another or challenges we are facing for the upcoming month. We are all professional women, and we started as a group to refer business to one another, but we have become so much more over the years.

One evening, the four of us sat and talked about travel we wanted to do. Reese said, "I want to travel more, but I just can't get away from work. I have saved enough money and invested well, but I cannot take time off." We started asking questions about her business structure, trying to offer solutions such as who could cover for her so she could take time off.

She stopped our feedback and said, "Let me be transparent: I become five years old again when it comes to money and looking at my budgets. I have enough to travel, I can take time off, and I could retire. But as Shannon recently reminded me, my money wounds from my childhood are preventing me from making the plans to slow down that would allow me to travel."

Lily jumped in. "I do not like to look at it either. I'm so glad my son is a wealth advisor. He will take care of me. My mother never knew about our family finances. My father was in control, and if too much money was spent, he would get really upset. I think that is why I don't like to even discuss money."

Then Kim chimed in. "Money was also controlled in my family. I decided from a young age that I would always work and maintain control financially. It has been what has driven me so intensely."

I found myself smiling at my friends. The conversation progressed for some time. Each of us, in turn, discussed our money-storied biases and dysfunctions. For me, it was a beautiful night. We had been meeting for years, talking about business, family, and hobbies, but we had never opened up about money in such a vulnerable way before. We agreed that our money experiences had profoundly impacted our lives, and we committed to supporting one another through our financial scar tissue to live the lives we truly wanted.

The differences between traditional and behavioral finance have only been actively studied since the 1980s. In recent years, the influence of behavioral finance has grown and challenged traditional thinking around money to help investors engage in better decision-making. The topic is becoming more popular, and I am seeing more research every year. The research is clear that without looking into our past experiences with money, we cannot fully understand our current relationship and may have great difficulty changing our future relationship. After thirty-plus years of working with real people, I am convinced that the behavioral side is even more important than the traditional one. We can learn about investments, but how we *emotionally* respond to money is usually underlying our actions.

Further Reflections

- What money scripts do you play regularly in your mind?
- Most of us have money biases—can you identify one of yours?
- As you read this chapter, in what ways did you think of your own past money experience?

Money Smarts

- Behavioral finance is what we do, consciously and unconsciously, because of our experiences with money.
- Each of us has our unique mix of emotions, blind spots, and influences that can radically change our outcomes with money.
- Money scripts are our unconscious beliefs around money.
- Money biases are our habitual responses to money.
- Money disorders go from mild to severe and can be as destructive as other addictions.

CHAPTER 3

The Social Media Game-Changer

Social media can be a source of bad financial advice,
impulsive purchases, peer pressure, and financial
stress. But responsible use can help you yield financial
gains and access learning and growth opportunities.

—MoneyGeek

At Princeton University on December 8, 2002, Daniel Kahneman gave a lecture that discussed his research showing we make financial decisions based 90 percent on emotion and only 10 percent on logic. That was more than two decades ago, well before the age of social media. Now, social media has created an online currency of likes, influencers, and curated imagery. How is that dynamic impacting our lives, our children, and our world? How is it impacting the financial decisions we make or how we feel about our own financial status?

Since 2007, we have all been glued to the small computers in our hands. Do not get me wrong—I love technology and the world it opens up. I relish thinking about all the beautiful minds we can access now that we are a more connected world. But I could have never imagined a world where we carry salespeople around in our hands, calling them influencers. It used to be that you would have to walk into a good old brick-and-mortar store to meet a salesperson. Now you can scroll through Instagram or TikTok and find hundreds of influencers selling you "the dream." My daughter loves makeup and follows many influencers who talk about the best products and how to apply them. She is always wanting—or should I say needing—new items! Some of these influencers have become very powerful and wealthy from selling us a lifestyle. How is this influencing our financial desires?

There is also a very personal aspect of social media. When we post and people make a comment or hit the "like" button, we feel like the world is cheering for us. It is a great dopamine hit! As Trevor Haynes said in a Harvard Education blog, "If you've ever misplaced your phone, you may have experienced a mild state of panic until it's been found. About 73% of people claim to experience this unique flavor of anxiety, which makes sense when you consider that adults in the US spend an average of two to four hours per day tapping, typing, and swiping on their devices—that adds up to over 2,600 daily touches."[1]

> If we understand that money is involved in achieving our human need for love, security, and acceptance, we can better understand the strength of the emotions we feel around our finances.

But we are also watching others, and it's hard to see someone posting something we desire but cannot afford or an accomplishment—such as an adult child getting offered a high-paying job—when our kid is financially struggling. It seems to me that this is having a profound impact on how we think about money;

it's changing our money behaviors to gain love, acceptance, and "likes." When it comes to our money and our values around money, we must be aware of all of the influences in our lives. If we understand that money is involved in achieving our human need for love, security, and acceptance, we can better understand the strength of the emotions we feel around our finances.

Why Do We Care What Others Think?

We care about what others think because one of our basic needs is love. If we are financially successful, we can provide more, and that makes us more attractive and therefore more eligible for love, in our society. Think about it: We have shows such as *Who Wants to Marry a Multi-Millionaire?* On Instagram, people do not post their ten-year-old cars; instead, they show off vacations, clothes, and new cars! We are fascinated with successful people, which almost always means financially successful. Such people are perceived as more intelligent and to be admired. We make shows and write books about them, and they have an influence on our society. We all want to know "how they did it."

There are many signs around us if we start to look. One is jewelry, which has been a sign of wealth for generations. We give rings with stones to ask for someone's hand in marriage. In some cultures, a large dowry of gold is presented. We are used to seeing lavish displays of wealth in estates, art, cars, planes, tennis shoes, and so many other products. Take a moment to notice all the displays of wealth you see daily. We care about what people think of our wealth because of the opportunities, admiration, and love that is extended to those who are perceived as financially successful.

Reflection

- What can you learn about yourself from the moments when you feel envious? Are there unmet needs or desires you should pay attention to?

- How might you shift your focus from comparing yourself to others on social media to appreciating your own journey and progress?

Are You Spending Money to Impress Other People?

If so, know you are not alone. At times, it's the surest fire way to feel like you belong. I clearly remember wanting Ditto jeans in junior high, and they were more expensive than my parents would pay for. So I babysat all summer to earn them. This was before I ever even tried them on! I wanted to fit in, wear cool jeans, and be part of the "in" group.

I cannot imagine that this will change in our lifetime; it's as old as time. I would like you to notice how fitting in influences how you handle your money.

A 2022 Bankrate poll found that one in three US adults with social media (34 percent) say they have felt negatively about their finances after seeing others' posts. Those feelings included jealousy, inadequacy, anxiety, shame, and anger. The poll went on to show that social media made users feel more pessimistic about their wallets than any other aspect of their lives, from appearances (32 percent) and careers (27 percent) to their living situations (26 percent), relationships (25 percent), and hobbies (17 percent).[2]

Do you feel pressure in your financial life from what you see on social media? My clients Dylan and Ashley did. We were working through their goals, and Ashley said, "I really think we should be traveling more." I remember being very aware of how she worded the statement—she used the word *should*. When I asked her to clarify, she said, "So many of our friends are posting their travel pictures that we feel like we should be as well. Although travel is not one of our primary goals at this time, the pressure to travel and post the pictures is very real to me." Her honesty was beautiful, allowing me to remind them of their stated goals. Extensive travel was not on their current goals list, and while they said that had not changed, the pressure of social media made them think that it might be the norm.

Reflection

- When you make a purchase, how often do you consider what others will think of it?

- How do you feel after making a purchase intended to impress others—satisfied, anxious, proud, or perhaps regretful?

- How can you celebrate your achievements and identity without relying on financial expenditures to express them?

Social Media Advice

In addition to being influenced to purchase, you'll encounter a frenzy of information on how to invest on social media. If you are thinking about a financial decision, you can find a lot of advice. But whose voice do you trust? Are you checking the source? Do you know how to check a source's actual knowledge?

Social media platforms have become popular sources for financial education, particularly among younger generations. Financial influencers on platforms like YouTube, TikTok, and Instagram provide accessible and often relatable financial advice. This can help improve financial literacy and inclusion, making complex financial concepts easier to understand and engage with.[3] There have been some positive impacts on financial literacy with the inception of social media. However, the quality of advice can vary, and there's a risk of encountering misinformation or unqualified advice, highlighting the need for critical evaluation and regulatory oversight.

For example, for years I worked out at a Pilates studio where the owner, Porter, was very vocal on her Instagram about investing. She had two huge studios and many employees whom she inspired. Porter ran a great business, and I enjoyed her studio model. Her posts were great, funny, motivating, and entrepreneurial in nature. Still, they started to concern me when she began giving stock tips and encouraged people not to miss out on Bitcoin purchases. She started weighing in on these investments regularly. She was successful and regularly showed her studios, her home with a pool, and her lifestyle of enjoying lavish meals and going out. I really think Porter was trying to motivate people to live their best lives! But in the process, she was influencing people that she did not know to buy very risky investments.

One morning right before I took a class, one of her instructors told me she had been investing in Bitcoin. She was excited, thinking about early retirement. It was going nowhere but up! What I knew about this Pilates instructor, Lauren, was that she rented an apartment, she had horrible car issues but not enough money to buy a new car, and she could barely afford the repairs. She did not have cash reserves, and she had talked about some additional debt. So why would Lauren risk money that she did not even have? Because she idolized Porter, wanted to be like her, and wanted to own the things Porter owned. I encouraged Lauren to pull out enough to pay off her debt, get a new car, and build a cash reserve while Bitcoin was at an all-time high. Did she do that? No, she watched it drop 84 percent, selling her positions for a considerable loss. She couldn't take the stress any longer. Porter still talks about the opportunity, but Lauren realized that the dream of early retirement or gym ownership for herself would not materialize overnight with Bitcoin. Defeated, Lauren returned to school to pursue an advanced degree in a field that would allow her to earn a higher income.

Was it Porter's fault? Absolutely not. She is not a licensed financial professional; she was on a public platform using freedom of speech. I think she was trying to help people. But Porter's influence changed one young woman's life, and I guess she wasn't the only one. I mute Porter's posts now, because it was hard for me to know her impact and continue to watch her financial "tips" to an unknown audience.

For full disclosure, I did my homework and researched Porter's background. I found no evidence or licensing to indicate she was an experienced financial professional. She was just sharing what was working for her and the risks she was taking. There are *thousands* of influencers in all areas of advice that impact our decision-making. When it comes to your money, beware of who you allow to influence you and your financial decisions.

Want to know if someone is licensed to talk about investing? Or is a trustworthy advisor? Try the Financial Industry Regulatory Authority's BrokerCheck and the Securities and Exchange Commission's Investment Adviser Public Disclosure websites. Checking your sources may not sound like fun, but having control over your financial life is empowering, and it is your responsibility to take care of yourself and your financial future.

Reflection

- What criteria do you use to determine if a social media source is trustworthy for financial advice?

- How do you manage feelings of inadequacy or FOMO (fear of missing out) that may arise from seeing others' financial successes online?

Cleaning Up Your Feed

You may mute rather than unfriend those whom you do not choose to be influenced by. People are the happiest when we align with their values. Unfollow those commercial accounts that entice you to purchase on a late-night scroll. You should also take the time to respond to ads and let social media know they are not relevant—simple and easy. This will take time, but soon you will find that your social media is no longer a place where you go to make unfair comparisons or unnecessary purchases.

Further Reflections

- Has social media ever influenced you financially?
- Do you ever get caught up in financial comparisons while viewing social media?

Money Smarts

- Social media has created an online currency of likes, influencers, and curated imagery.
- With financial decisions often based on emotion, social media's influence is a game-changer.
- Clean up your social media feed so you don't see posts that may be causing you to compare yourself financially or influence unnecessary purchases.
- Investment advice through a social media scroll is an advertisement, not a hot tip!

CHAPTER 4

Aligning Your Money and Values

The way you manage your money reflects the things
you care about the most. Align your financial decisions
with your core values, and you will find fulfillment.

—Manisha Thakor, *On My Own Two Feet*

H ave you heard the saying "Follow the money, and you will see what someone values"? How we use our money does tell a story, but what story does yours tell? Is it in alignment with your values, or does it reflect your money scripts or what you thought you *should* do with your money? This is a tricky question, but it's one of the most important I ask in this book. We fail to reach money satisfaction when we are unclear about what we value. Aligning your financial decisions with your personal values leads to greater satisfaction and fulfillment. When spending and investing reflect your core beliefs and priorities, it enhances your sense of purpose and happiness.[1]

I was once asked to talk, as one of the keynote speakers at a women's conference, about money and how it aligns with our values. About four hundred women were in the audience as I discussed aligning their goals with their values.

As I finished my presentation, a woman close to the front raised her hand. "Shannon, I understand what you're saying," she said, "but my greatest desire is to pay for my son's college education. I just can't afford to do that."

"I understand," I responded. "Education is very, very expensive. Your son can apply for scholarships and loans and grants."

"No," she said, shaking her head. "That's my number one goal. What I want to do is to pay for 100 percent of my son's education."

I asked her to see me afterward, and at the end of my presentation, I invited her to join me back in the green room. She introduced herself as Sara, then repeated that she couldn't afford to pay for her son's college.

"I believe that's what you're telling yourself," I answered, "but let's find out for sure." I asked her to tell me a little bit about herself.

She told me she had lived in South Bay for the last thirty years, a fairly wealthy area in Southern California. She said she owned her home outright—in fact, she was very proud that she had just made her last mortgage payment. She told me she was a widow. Her husband had passed suddenly several years earlier, and she was now on a fixed income with very little in savings.

I knew about home values in her area, and I was fairly sure she had enough equity in her house to pay for her son's college education easily. She could take money out of her home with an equity loan or even sell if she chose to and downsize. I asked her if she'd considered remortgaging the house.

My question shocked her. "Why would I do that? I just paid it off!"

"Sara, I think finally having your home paid off has been one of your top financial goals."

"No," she answered, clearly frustrated. "My goal is to pay for my son's education."

"Are you sure that's what you want?" I asked. "It seems to me that you want the security of a paid-off home, and you have the right to have that. So, congratulations again! Consider what would happen if you stopped telling yourself that your number-one financial goal is paying for your son's education. I think you have it within your means to do that, either with a mortgage or by selling your house. You seem closed off to that option—and that's okay, but you're making yourself miserable."

Sara was silent; she appeared to be thinking through what I'd just said. I went on, "I suggest you help your son apply for every scholarship and help him research loans and grants. Help him consider saving money by going to a community college for the first two years before he transfers to a four-year university. There's a lot you can do to help."

Suddenly, a lightness came over her. "You're right," she said. "I need the security of having my home paid off. I want to know that, on my fixed income, I'll always have a place to live."

She acknowledged that she had been focused on her son's education because she felt it was the right thing to do. Since he was in nursery school, she heard other parents from her wealthy neighborhood talk about how their children's college funds were growing. Now she understood that he needed her guidance more than her money. This realization seemed to bring her some clarity. She could still help her son navigate college costs and stay true to what was most important to her. Her finances were in alignment with her values. She appeared a little less burdened when she gave me a hug, expressing her gratitude.

> ## Reflection
>
> - Is there a goal you have, like Sara did, that may be out of alignment?
> - In what ways do your current financial habits reflect (or not reflect) your values?

Discover Your Financial Values

Aligning values and financial behavior is critical in achieving long-term financial goals. By engaging in disciplined behaviors like budgeting, saving, and investing, individuals can improve their financial health and achieve milestones such as homeownership, retirement, and education.[2] So, how do you set your financial values? Let's first establish what I mean by financial values. I like the definition from the *Cambridge Dictionary*: "the beliefs people have, especially about what is right and wrong and what is most important in life, that control their behavior."[3]

Many people firmly believe that money is not something you should value. I find a lot of guilt and shame emerges when I ask about financial values. Why? Society, at least here in the United States, has taught us that what we value should not be money, or that valuing money makes you a bad person. It reminds me of that 1987 movie, *Wall Street*, where the main character famously said, "Greed is good."[4] In the 1990s, there was a cultural shift, with many rejecting this idea, calling greed "bad." However, when I discuss values, I'm not talking about greed or the love of money.

Most of us are motivated to act one way or another toward

the things we value. We have basic human needs, such as eating, drinking clean water, shelter, and clothing. If we are fortunate to have resources beyond our basic human needs, then we make daily choices regarding spending, saving, or investing our money. What motivates these choices? Have you ever really thought about the why behind how you spend your discretionary income? Here's where the values part comes in: If you look at where you are actually spending your money, you will see what you value—or *think* you should value.

Reflection

- How well do your current spending habits align with your core values?

- What are the top three to five values that are most important to you in life?

- In what areas of your life would you like to allocate more financial resources in order to better align with your values?

How Do You Determine Your Values?

1. Identify: Make a list of your top money values.

2. Prioritize: From that list, choose your top three—the ones that mean the most to you.

3. Know your why: Next to your top three values, write down why they are the most important to you.

Do you need help? Sometimes it takes work to think about what we value regarding money. Many of us have a strong voice in our heads that tells us what we should value. Try to push that voice aside or tell it to be quiet momentarily. That voice can be your past experiences with family or your community. It can limit you by keeping you in "shoulds" or shame around money.

Here is a list of values I hear from clients that may prompt you to identify yours:

1. Financial security/building wealth
2. College education of children and grandchildren
3. Retirement or financial independence
4. Experiences—travel
5. Paying off consumer debt and staying out of debt
6. Philanthropic—wanting to donate money to support meaningful nonprofit work
7. Buying a home or a second home

Whatever you want or value should be *unique to your life experience.* I will never forget my client Mary, who was referred to me after her husband died. She was in her late seventies. They had owned a bike shop in a beach city in Southern California and worked hard their whole lives with very few extras. But they had created a comfortable retirement, and after her husband died she wanted help to manage that retirement. When Mary first came into my office, we started by discussing her needs, her cost of living (her monthly and annual expenses), her values around money, and where she spends her money.

It became clear to me that Mary was very budget-conscious. She had some repairs she needed to do on her home, but beyond that she was content. She did not want to travel, and she just wanted to spend time with grandchildren who lived close to her. I noticed something, though: Every meeting, she came into my office clutching a designer purse, and she kept it close to her. It was well-worn, but it was evident it meant a lot to her.

At our next meeting, I complimented her on the purse and asked her about it. She lit up as she told me that it was a gift from her husband for her fiftieth birthday. She had always wanted this designer bag but never felt it was prudent to purchase such a luxury. When her husband surprised her for her birthday, she said it was the best gift she had ever received. After she lost her husband, it served as a reminder of his love. She went on to say that it was now quite worn after twenty years. She wanted to buy a new one from the same designer brand but could not bring herself to make the purchase. She valued the purse and what it meant to her. However, she felt ashamed that she valued a material item, and she said she didn't want to purchase a new one.

After putting together a plan and ensuring that Mary had the resources she needed to live and cover her cost of living, I let Mary know she had plenty of money to make discretionary choices. She was also very active in her church and wanted to continue to tithe, so she was thrilled she had enough to give to others. I also let her know that she could buy a new purse—not to replace the well-loved one her husband had given her, but one to give the treasured purse a rest. She loved the idea and promised me she would buy a new purse.

Over the course of the next ten years, Mary still came into my office with the same worn purse. She would ask me if it was still okay to buy a new one, I would assure her it was, and she would leave planning her purchase. The last time I saw Mary, she still carried the old purse. I offered to go to the store with her, as she was now starting to not feel well, and her time appeared to be more limited. She left my office again excited and promising to purchase a new purse.

About six months later, I received a call from her daughter Rose to let me know Mary had passed. As Rose was in the house, I asked her to do me a favor, and she agreed. I asked her to look in her mom's closet for the purse her father had purchased. Rose went into Mary's room and said, "Shannon, the purse is here, but there is also a new one that's very similar. Mom must have just purchased it." I started to get misty-eyed, and I told Rose about what the purses meant to her mom, and said I hoped she and her sister would cherish them.

How can a purse be something one values? To Mary, it was a symbol of love from her husband. It was an extravagance she did not expect but enjoyed tremendously. One of life's gifts is allowing ourselves to enjoy an extravagance we can afford. Too often, we restrict ourselves to not making a purchase we would like because it feels frivolous, we are afraid it would look bad to others, or we think we cannot afford it. Aligning your money with your values is a personal decision. To take control of your financial life, you must determine what you value without judgment or shame.

Reflection

- Looking back, are there financial decisions you've made that didn't align with your values? What can you learn from those experiences?

- What support or resources do you need to help you stay committed to a values-driven financial approach?
- How can you celebrate your progress when you make financial decisions that reflect your values?

Live in Alignment

When do you know that you are financially in alignment with your desires? You will feel happier; your stress level will be low and your financial outlook will be confident. Really. Many times over my career, I have wished for a magic wand to help people, but I have found that they've had it the whole time but were not using it. The simplicity of creating goals that are in alignment with your values and then creating habits to achieve those goals sounds simple. And it is, but it's not easy because of all the financial scar tissue. Those

> Aligning your money with your values is a personal decision. To take control of your financial life, you must determine what you value without judgment or shame.

relentless voices in our heads are full of shame and shoulds. There's a reason I've taken the first four chapters to discuss the emotional side of money: Life is less about what the world hands to us than how we react to it.

This is the part where you need to give yourself some grace. It may have taken you years to create your financial life, career, house, car, possessions, investments, and spending habits. It will take time, maybe years, to get to the point where you are truly living in financial alignment with your values. After decades of working with people, I have found that the mental shift goes quicker than you think, and once you have changed the way you look at money in this world and how you want to interact with it, it will be a force moving you forward into alignment.

Further Reflections

- What are your top money values?
- Are you living financially in alignment with those values?
- Is there something that is really important to you that you cannot "afford"?

Money Smarts

- We only reach money satisfaction when we know what we value.
- Values reflect your own assessments of what is important in your life and with your money.
- To take control of your financial life, you must determine what you value without judgment or shame.

CHAPTER 5

Financial Wounds and Their Origins

Use pain as a stepping stone,
not a campground.

—Alan Cohen

My memory is unclear on when I started noticing patterns of financial wounds, but I clearly remember when I started to ask about financial biases. I have been aware of the behavioral side of money from a very young age, as I've shared. But it took me years to get the courage to ask direct questions of clients to try to help them identify where their money beliefs came from.

When I started as a financial advisor, there were thirty new advisors in my class. Two of us were women. At the time, it was not uncommon for potential new clients to tell me that they would love to work with me, but they would be more comfortable working with a man. To me, that meant I needed to steer clear of talking about "soft" topics, such as emotions, as they were considered a more feminine characteristic at that time. I decided to stay more formal, less emotional, and be the best I could be at investing. It worked, and my practice grew quickly. I got my CFP and continued to add credentials.

I set aside my knowledge and interest in behavioral finance for years, thinking that it was too emotional and not wanting to intrude into such a personal space and make someone uncomfortable. Talking about emotions around money was not what the industry was doing. The focus was talking about hot stock tips and individual stocks, and I fell into many of the same expectations and focused primarily on great returns. I did financial plans with all of my clients, and I was proud of the comprehensive work around all areas of my clients' financial lives, but the real interest of most of the clients was where I was going to invest their money and what kind of returns they would get. This focus on returns is logical because it's how we measure successful investing. But the question that plagued me day in and day out was: Are we looking for the right outcome?

The day I really started asking about financial memories started like every other day. I had five client meetings in my office. The portfolio reviews were prepared and sat in folders on my desk with each of the clients' names on the tabs. My first clients that day were a couple who had just retired; they were in their early seventies. We had been working together for the last couple of years to get them prepared financially to retire, and their primary goal in retirement was travel. When Ann and Franklin walked into my office, I immediately knew there was something wrong. It was as if a cloud of sadness walked in with this normally optimistic couple. We sat down at the table with their review folder in the middle of the table. I placed my hand on the folder and said, "I am looking forward to reviewing the investment returns with you, but before we get started, please let me know how you would like to focus our time today."

Ann immediately started to cry. She was sobbing so hard I couldn't understand what she was saying. Franklin took her hand, looked at me, and said, "I have been diagnosed with stage 4 cancer—it's aggressive." Franklin cleared his voice and went on, "And I am angry, not just because I have cancer but because I focused on work all these years when Ann wanted me to start traveling with her earlier. I could have, but the pressure of earning money for retirement seemed more important. Now I may not live to travel, and if I do, we may be restricted by my physical ability."

Ann added, "I'm scared; I didn't plan on being a caregiver but a travel partner. These were meant to be our golden years. Why did we wait? Why did I agree to wait?"

The pain in both of their voices was heart-wrenching. They had great careers, had built a strong retirement portfolio, and got competitive returns on that portfolio. But all of that seemed to be a lot less important considering this news. Great investments and money were not going to change the fact that Franklin now had stage 4 cancer with a grim prognosis. All of my pride in how I had managed their portfolio quickly flowed out of me, and it was replaced by a deep sense of questioning what I do for clients. I knew that travel was their number one goal, Ann had been begging Franklin to travel earlier in their lives together, and they could have afforded to do so. Why didn't I ask what was holding Franklin back from traveling or retiring earlier? They could have done both, but my hesitation in getting too emotional with clients had stopped me. Had I just been playing it safe by focusing on the investment returns? But that's what my clients wanted, right?

After Franklin and Ann left the office, I looked at the remaining four folders, and at that moment I made the decision that I would dig deeper and ask harder questions—not just talk about the amount of money someone had accumulated or their rates of return, but what the money was *for*, what kind of life they wanted to create with the financial savings they worked so hard to accumulate.

Once I started asking questions—"What is important to you financially? What did you learn from your family or community about money?"—patterns of financial wounds started to emerge. Franklin's drive-to-work-and-then-enjoy-retirement attitude is something I now can recognize in speech patterns. I hear it expressed as "I just need to make sure our retirement is fully funded, then I can enjoy a trip or two" and "My father worked until seventy, never took a day off, and provided well for our family." It is often a level of responsibility that is admirable but can create pressure for the primary income earner or a couple not to enjoy the fruits of their labor until retirement. But what if retirement, the way you picture it, never comes? Can the financial wounds of responsibility and expectation cause us to fall short of our dreams? Absolutely.

When I started in this industry, I thought it was about investing. What I have learned is that impactful financial planning means overcoming financial wounds, because the expectations we have created around money may not align with our dreams. Digging into the soft side of money, the emotional questions, the fear, and the dreams is a far more effective way of living a financially happy life than just watching our investment returns.

Reflection

- How do you define financial success? Is it purely about numbers, or does it include other aspects of well-being?

> • What would financial peace of mind look like for you beyond just having enough money?

The Origins of Financial Wounds

Identifying your wounds means reminding yourself that they are not a permanent part of your financial life; they are a part of your past you can choose to heal and move on from. Before you become aware of your wounds, you developed a bias or became predisposed to thoughts that repeated over and over. All of this limited your ability to find financial happiness. Once you recognize the wounds, you become able to respond in light of them rather than unconsciously reacting to the scar tissue that formed around them. This process may take a great deal of work; it may take professional help. I'm not saying you will wake up one day and everything will be new and easy. However, once you know, you have the ability to do better for yourself.

> Identifying your wounds means reminding yourself that they are not a permanent part of your financial life; they are a part of your past you can choose to heal and move on from.

Where do these wounds come from? For most of us, they come from deeply seated beliefs we've absorbed from our families, our communities, or our cultural backgrounds. Sometimes we can identify the pain point easily when the wound or bias comes out of trauma, such as power being abused around money, but most often they come from others' beliefs around money that we have adopted as our truth. They cause us pain because they are not in alignment with our personal desires. Until we identify the origin of the wounds or bias, we can unconsciously continue to make decisions around money that do not make us happy. We continually ask why we keep making the same money mistakes.

Reflection

- Looking back, are there specific financial wounds you can identify as being particularly impactful? How have they shaped your financial life?

- How have you tried to cope with or heal from your financial wounds? What strategies have been effective, and which ones haven't?

Financial Wound or Deeply Imbedded Belief?

To this point, we have talked a lot about the money experiences that have created memories. For example, growing up in a financially stable or unstable environment can influence our sense of financial security and risk tolerance in adulthood.[1] Now, please consider that some of your financial scar tissue may not have arisen from a traumatic experience, but rather from a set of beliefs you have embedded into how you think about money, instilled by the community you were raised in, how your parents handled money, or how someone you admired talked about money. Experiences of all types work to create a set of beliefs about how we see the world, and money is no different.

We all have subconscious things we do on autopilot in our lives, and money is no exception. Are you financially happy? Do you feel restricted financially by a set of rules you live by or unfulfilled by your financial goals? It may be time to explore what wounds or embedded beliefs you are carrying around. So often when you can identify these *shoulds* you have been carrying for years—maybe even generations in your family—you can find the freedom to approach your financial life with a new perspective.

Reflection

- How can you reframe your past financial experiences to view them as lessons rather than wounds?
- What positive financial habits can you develop to counteract the effects of past financial wounds?

Getting Uncomfortable

I am a big fan of getting uncomfortable. It's when we put ourselves under stress that we often grow, and in that growth we can find what is truly most important to us. However, I have found that not everyone is comfortable with change. Some of the greatest struggles I have witnessed around money are not people getting uncomfortable with their decisions, facing their wounds, and making a new path. Instead it's often the reaction of family and friends. Remember my story about Allison and John in chapter 1? They wanted to travel, not own a home that used up all their discretionary income and prevented them from traveling.

They were thrilled with their decision to sell the larger home to buy a more affordable home so they could afford to travel. What I did not share was the criticism they endured from parents around this choice. Their parents told them that their choice to buy a smaller home and travel was frivolous, selfish, and a bad decision. Twenty years later, I can share that Allison and John have not regretted that decision. However, they have endured a lot of back-handed comments at family gatherings. They, like so many clients I have worked with, have learned that the negativity often comes from fear and disappointment that others have around their own unexamined financial lives.

Further Reflections

- What is a money thought you ruminate on? When did it start?
- Who in your life had the most influence on how you think about money?
- Would you say your family was financially healthy or unhealthy in their money beliefs?
- What society or community pressures do you feel about money?

Money Smarts

- Wounds often come from deep-seated beliefs that we absorb from our families, communities, or cultural backgrounds.
- Identifying your wounds is to remind yourself that they are not a permanent part of your financial life.
- Financial wounds cause pain because they are not in alignment with our personal desires.
- Financial negativity often comes from fear and disappointment in an unexamined financial life.

CHAPTER 6

Planning for Your Goals

Your goals are the blueprints to your life. When you
set them with intention, they shape your path and
help you stay focused on what really matters.

—Brian Tracy

"**W**hat are your most important money goals?" I have
asked this question of clients for thirty years. The
most common response I get is, "I have never really
thought about that" or "No one has ever asked me that." This is a
profound question that catches people off guard. After learning
this during many silent, awkward meetings, I now encourage people to give some thought to the question before our meeting. Why
is this such a tricky question? I think it's because our heads are so
full of expectations from our family or society that we do not take
the time to answer it authentically for ourselves.

Daniel and Kristin quietly fidgeted in their chairs across from
me. They had been very talkative on the way into our meeting,
their investment portfolio statements in their hands. They had
been referred to me by a friend, and they seemed excited to start

planning for their financial future. After we sat down, I asked, "What is most important to you about money?"

Daniel quickly answered, "As you can see, we have been saving. We have 401(k)s, IRAs, no debt, and a cash reserve. Those statements have all the details."

I placed my hand on the statements. Rather than opening them up to look at account balances or holdings, I pushed them to the side of the table, away from Daniel and Kristin. I said, "Yes, thank you, we will get to these statements. But first, what is most important to you about money?"

That's when the silence fell and the fidgeting began. Kristin finally said, "Well, we want to retire. We just need to know if we have enough money to retire by sixty."

"Retirement is an exciting time, and sixty is early," I replied. "Tell me about what you are retiring *to*."

Daniel said, "We're just tired of working and want to retire as early as possible." He gestured toward the paperwork. I could tell I was making him uncomfortable. They had come in for me to calculate their numbers and give them the freedom to declare that retirement would be achieved in the next couple of years. I wasn't *trying* to frustrate them, but I knew that without a clear understanding of what was important to them and their money values in retirement, they might not find the satisfaction they were looking for by simply having enough money.

By focusing the planning on the outcome—the goal—of retirement, I was able to help Daniel and Kristin align their hard-earned resources with the lifestyle they really wanted, which wasn't just an escape from work. They both did retire early from their corporate jobs, but they decided they would do some consulting to create additional income with flexible hours to

support the extensive travel they wanted to do, which had been beyond their initial retirement plans.

Like Daniel and Kristin, you may find yourself wanting to "escape" a job or current financial reality. But to do so, you may compromise what you really want. In fact, with Daniel and Kristin, initially they would not even allow themselves to talk about the travel they really wanted to do because of the overwhelming desire they felt to quit the jobs they were in. By exploring their goals in a deeper way, not just their account balances, we had the opportunity to look at options to get them out of their corporate jobs, still earn some money, and have the freedom to do the travel they deeply wanted to do.

I Want, I Want, I Want

Children often have what I call the "I want, I want, I wants," but as we get older, after being told "no" for years, if not decades, it's often difficult to allow ourselves the freedom to think about our authentic desires. We get wrapped up in what we believe is possible, what we *should* be doing, or what we *need* to own. But what if you took all those expectations—which often come from influencers, family, friends, social media, community, or yourself—and released them?

In the summer of 2023, *Barbie* was a big hit movie. My daughter Taylor has always been very "girlie"—in fact, we have been calling her "Little Miss" since a very young age. The "Barbie Summer" was a dream for her! Many of her favorite brands had Barbie merchandise collaborations. For months she had been eyeing a Barbie-pink suitcase line that was a very limited production. She missed the first round. But in July, on a hot summer day as we headed down the mountain from our family cabin in the woods to do some laundry and gather some supplies, Little Miss screamed with excitement as we got back into cell coverage. She was notified that her luggage set would be restocked in a few days, and she would have the first opportunity to purchase! Taylor was a junior in high school at the time. She had been working as a hostess at a national restaurant chain and had been saving her money. She needed new luggage, and this was the opportunity she had been waiting for. The luggage set was bright pink with a beautiful lining. It came with three pieces and an expensive price tag.

I assured her that if she took the time to think through the purchase over the next couple of days and the true "cost" of using her hard-earned money on these suitcases, I would drive back down the mountain into cell coverage with her to purchase if that was her decision.

Over the next couple of days, we enjoyed hikes, water sports, and the beach as we continued our conversation around purchasing the Barbie suitcases. We talked through the same questions we did on many of our family purchases: "What about the suitcases is special to you? You had to work more than three weeks of shifts to earn enough money, after taxes, to make this purchase—was that time worth this purchase? If you do not buy them, what else could you use the money for? They are bright pink; do you think you will use them for several years or grow tired of the color?" We had many casual conversations, and Taylor spoke to my sisters about her excitement as well and why she wanted to purchase the luggage.

My sister Lisa was taken aback by all the discussion around pink suitcases. She told me her initial thought was *What are you thinking? Those are too expensive! I would never let my daughters purchase those, even with their own money.* I was not surprised by this reaction, as both my sisters and I had been raised by our parents to be very practical in our purchasing choices. Lisa went on to tell me how amazed she was at how Taylor and I were discussing the purchase, how I was guiding her to make the best choice for her. She acknowledged that she, too, had loved purses and girly things growing up, but to this day, she often had buyer's remorse, even when she could afford a purchase. We had a great conversation about the financial expectations we had grown up with and the wounds we still lived with around money. Three days later, Taylor was certain, and we drove just far enough down the mountain into cell coverage to order the suitcases with her hard-earned money.

It took a couple of months to receive the suitcases, and my sister Lisa just happened to be in our city visiting after a business conference when the bags arrived. She was able to experience the unencumbered joy that Taylor had when opening her new set of luggage. We were all giddy with excitement over every detail and of Taylor's well-made financial decision.

> ### Reflection
>
> - What are some *shoulds* you have accepted without questioning, and how do they influence your behavior?
> - What fears or consequences hold you back from rejecting the *should* in favor of pursuing what you truly want?
> - What small step can you take today to challenge a *should* in your life?

What Do You Really Desire?

You've likely heard the age-old question, "What would you do if money were not a concern?" To me, this is a tricky question, because money is *always* a concern for most of us. But if you think about the heart of the question, it asks you to find your true north. What is meant by "true north?" The phrase *discover your true north* was coined by Harvard Business School professor and author Bill George in his best-selling book.[1] It is your inner sense of what you want to accomplish. It's the alignment of your values, dreams, and resources.

What is your true north? Earlier, I shared several stories of clients who felt they were following their heart's greatest desire only to discover it was an expectation someone else had put on them, and they adapted. Allison and John wanted to travel but were "house poor." Tara had a fear of running out of money. It took some work, but in both cases, these clients found their internal money compass versus being driven by the external pressure or fear.

Financial goals support not only financial stability but also contribute to overall life satisfaction by aligning financial practices

> Find your true north. What do you want for yourself?

with personal values and life goals. This holistic approach ensures that money is used as a tool to enhance life quality rather than being an end in itself. Outlining your goals and dreams is also one of the most rewarding parts of financial planning. What do you want for yourself? When you act in alignment with your objectives, your true north, that's when the money happiness starts.

Foundational Steps for Planning for Your Goals

1. Create clarity around what are your most important financial goals.

2. Outline your goals by determining the cost and timing.

3. Review your discretionary income (the money beyond your fixed expenses). You must know what you can save monthly/annually toward your goals.

4. Eliminate any goals that are not in alignment with your values.

5. Revisit your goals regularly to measure progress.

If your goal is important to you, track it. The best way to do this is to hire an advisor or a coach to hold you accountable and push you. Yes, I am biased, but the data agrees: Statistically, people who meet regularly with their professional financial advisors reach their goals more often.

Even the savviest investors doubt their decisions. They can run out of time or feel lost among all the choices in the market-place. Having a partner, coach, or financial advisor to help guide you through decisions and keep you on track by simply meeting a couple of times a year can significantly impact your ability to achieve your goals.

Advisors are not just for the wealthy. There is a wide variety of advisors, and many do not have a minimum amount of wealth you must have to invest with them. Having some structured method of revisiting your goals with a knowledgeable advisor who can offer ideas, strategy, and encouragement can benefit you regardless of how much wealth you possess right now.

If you choose to go it alone, structure your time to review goals and research options and strategies. This approach can be just as effective as working with a wealth manager, but only if it is done consistently. The key here is that this kind of review is not a one-and-done. Revisit your goals over time and through various economic environments if you want to be successful in the long term.

Further Reflections

- What is your true north, your most important desires for your life?

- Are there any external pressures preventing you from these goals?

- Do you have recurring thoughts about money that are limiting your ability to create your financial goals?

Money Smarts

- Identify your most important money goals.

- Know why your financial goals are important; challenge the why behind each goal.

- Enlist your partner, a coach, or a financial advisor to help you stay on track with your stated desires.

PART II

Building Your Financial Foundation

CHAPTER 7

Cost of Living

Too many people spend money they haven't
earned, to buy things they don't want,
to impress people that they don't like.

—Will Rogers

O nce you know what you want and are clear on your goals,
how do you get started? Over the next few chapters, I
will introduce you to the essentials when it comes to
managing your money and what I feel are the *key* things to think
about. There is a wealth of financial planning information you can
easily find to create a deeper understanding. These chapters are
meant to help you create a method to align your resources with
your personal values in a simple, straightforward way. They will
help you alter your financial behavior—this is where the financial
rubber meets the road.

What Is Your Cost of Living?

When someone finds out what I do for a living, I often get two
questions: "How much money do I need to retire?" and "How

much should I invest annually?" Both questions are tough because we are all unique. Each of you reading may have a different cost of living. We live in different places in the world with differing access to goods and services, which will often dictate our basic cost of living—housing, food, clothing, transportation, health care, and so on. Someone who lives in New York City is more likely to have a higher cost of living than someone who lives in Missouri. *Your* cost of living will be the basis on which you determine what you will need to save in order to retire or invest annually for other goals. There are other factors, such as inflation and taxation, that you need to consider as well, but that's for a more detailed financial planning book or to address during your meeting with a financial advisor. The purpose of this chapter is to help you understand what it costs you to live today on a monthly and annual basis.

Amanda, a single woman, had been referred to me by another client. "Shannon, I'm almost forty, and I'm realizing that a financial Prince Charming is not coming," she joked. "I'm starting to do this adulting thing, and I really need to put together a better investment plan." After having a good laugh over wanting to be rescued so she did not have to think about money, I shared with her that one of the scariest and most empowering things we can realize in life is that no one is coming to save us financially.

As we started to roll up our sleeves on her cash flow, I quickly realized that most of Amanda's monthly cash flow went to credit cards and other debt. She had a strong income and had stashed some money in a 401(k) at work but had very little in cash reserves. I asked Amanda what was important to her about money. What was she trying to accomplish?

"You know," she replied, "I really am at the point where I feel that I need to get my credit cards paid off. I need to build a cash reserve, and I think I need to start saving for retirement—maybe even for a house. I've just waited so long. I've been traveling and really enjoying myself, but I think it's time to get serious."

I asked her to tell me about her cash flow: What money came in and what went out? Her body language told me she did not like the question. She looked right at me and said, "Shannon, ignorance is bliss. If I don't budget, I don't track what I'm spending or know where it's going. I can just enjoy my life. If I start to track it, I realize that I'm spending money on things I shouldn't, and I just hide. It's too uncomfortable. I work really hard every day, and I deserve to have some fun."

I told her I understood but reminded her that she had mentioned some very specific goals. I explained that her credit card debt was a warning sign she might be spending beyond what she was bringing home. I asked her to picture herself *without* the heavy credit card debt and *with* a cash reserve that allowed her not to live paycheck-to-paycheck. Amanda agreed that it would be nice, but in her mind this meeting was still about an investment plan. She started to push me for investment ideas, wanting to know where to invest the small amount of savings she *did* have so it could grow quickly. We were living in the age of Bitcoin, and she wanted a quick fix or a stock tip.

Rather than discussing investment ideas at this stage, I asked to see all of Amanda's primary checking account bank accounts for the last year. We went over them, month by month. I wanted to understand what she was bringing home and what she was spending. I needed to help her figure out why she was adding credit card debt every year. More importantly, were those credit card purchases in alignment with her goals and values, or was she just spending frivolously on things that weren't important?

It soon became clear that she was overspending what she was bringing home by about $300 per month. That habit caught up with her when she had unplanned expenses, such as a refrigerator repair or a veterinarian bill for her cat. The money that should have been growing her cash reserve was paying those credit card bills.

We identified her core expenses each month (rent, food, car, clothing) and then started layering in her discretionary expenses. She was surprised to find that she had about $600 a month available after core expenses.

That discretionary spending was where the problems started: She was going out for drinks with friends, taking weekend trips, buying extra clothes, and going out to lunch most days (and dinner some nights) because she lived alone and didn't like to eat by herself. Those costs were adding up much quicker than she realized.

"Well, maybe ignorance isn't bliss, Shannon," she admitted. "Some of these things don't bring me any joy, and I'm going into debt for them."

Once she could see where her money was actually going each month, Amanda started making decisions that aligned better with *her* values. She still likes going out to lunch and having drinks with friends. She still takes weekend trips. But now she's aware of the cost—and not just the dollar value of the item or experience, but what it costs her in potential savings and credit card debt payments.

It took about a year for Amanda to get her cash reserves built up and her credit cards paid off. Life still sent her emergencies and opportunities while she tried to pay down her credit card debt, so we worked on building up her cash cushion at the same time she was paying down the debt.

Amanda created a budget based on her core expenses, then decided how to allocate that extra $600 a month. She had only been paying the minimums on her credit cards and was tempted to pay them off quickly. But I was concerned that she might fall back into old habits once the balances were lower, thinking, *I'm working hard, and I deserve it.*

Instead, I encouraged her to put equal amounts of money each month into her cash reserves and her credit card debt. She decided to spend less on eating out, too, which gave her an extra $250 a month in her budget.

Once Amanda got in the swing of it, she was able to increase what she was saving and how much she was paying off on her credit cards. She got it all done within a year, and without that credit card burden, her monthly discretionary money went from $600 to $850.

Amanda said she felt like a weight had been lifted from her. When friends asked her to go away for a weekend, she knew she had the cash to pay for it without going into revolving credit card debt.

She now had enough money to start working on her long-term goals. Amanda wanted to save for a home and also put money away for her retirement, so we set her up on a plan to do both. We talked about investment strategies, but our conversation was based on a solid financial footing this time.

Now, Amanda says that being on a budget makes her feel like she has more freedom than she's ever had. Understanding what money is coming in and going out makes her feel in control. She makes decisions in alignment with the things that make her truly happy. This is no surprise. A significant number of people adhere to a budget. According to a survey by Debt.com, more than 80 percent of Americans report having a monthly budget, a trend that has been increasing over the past six years.[1] This indicates a growing awareness and practice of budgeting among the population. However, there is often a gap between having a budget and sticking to it consistently. *Social desirability bias is a well-documented phenomenon that leads individuals to over-report positive behaviors, including financial practices like budgeting, while under-reporting less favorable behaviors, such as failure to adhere to a budget.*[2]

Ten years later, Amanda owns her own home. She's married and saving for her kids' education. She never went back to being in credit card debt. When I meet with her and her husband, we have a good laugh about the notion that ignorance is bliss. The first step is to know what you are spending.

Reflection

- Have you accurately assessed your cost of living and what factors (such as fixed expenses, lifestyle choices, and unexpected costs) you might be overlooking when calculating your monthly budget?

- What fears, habits, or beliefs might be preventing you from honestly examining your true cost of living, and how could these factors be influencing your financial decisions or overall sense of security?

Budget versus Run Rate

You are unique in how you spend money monthly and annually. You have different fixed costs (housing, cars, insurance, medical, and food) and discretionary costs (entertainment, clothing, travel, and dining out) from everyone else. Before you start to invest or plan for retirement or a college education for your kids, you need to establish your cost of living, often referred to as your budget. However, I rarely use the word *budget* with clients, as it immediately evokes a feeling of being restricted. I find this approach often triggers them to feel guilt around spending on items they worry others (including me as their advisor) would think are frivolous. As a result, if you start to write down what you think you are spending in a budget format, you will often come up with a much smaller number than you are *really* spending. I encourage people to instead think of this same number as their "run rate"—what it costs you to live monthly and annually.

Often we underestimate nonrecurring expenses such as gift-giving, emergencies, and travel. We chalk them up to

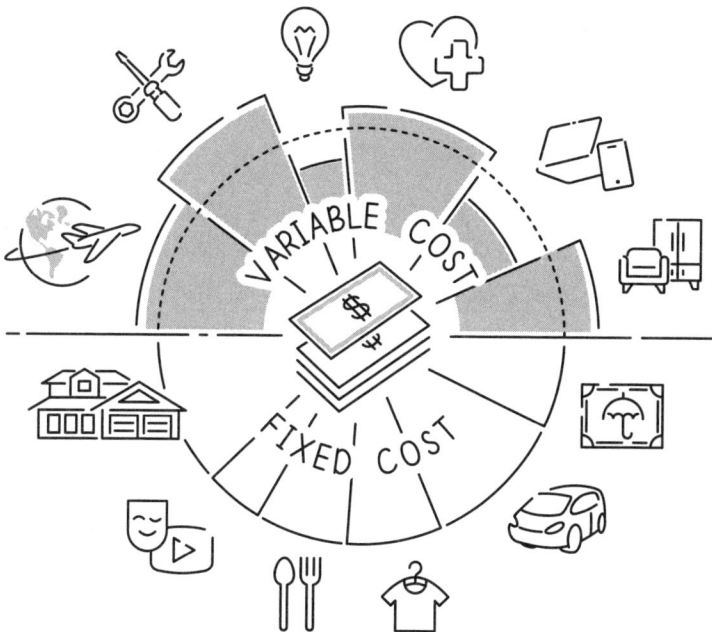

one-time occurrences. The best way I have found is to figure out your cost of living, or run rate, by looking at the bank account you use to pay bills. Often a household will deposit checks into an account and then pay bills and credit cards and withdraw cash. If you take your statements for one year and look at what your income was and what you spent, you will start to see a pattern. Some months will be higher—maybe you have property taxes, need new tires for the car, or it's a holiday season. Looking at your cost of living this way, you get a more accurate accounting of what you are spending. To dig in deeper, look at the line items. I find that most people do most of their spending using credit cards, electronic payment methods, or checks. These statements will tell the story of where you are spending money. When my husband and I started this exercise with my daughters, they were surprised at how quickly the drive-thru and coffee charges, which seemed small, added up.

Why put yourself through this painful exercise? If you have financial goals, you need to know what you have to save toward those goals and what those goals may cost. Retirement is the example I used earlier. When someone asks me how much money they will need to retire, I am only able to answer that question if I know what they will be spending in retirement. Again, we all spend money in different ways, we live in different parts of the world, and we have a wide variety of costs of living. By establishing what you will spend during retirement before you retire, you can make a more accurate prediction of what you may need in savings long term.

Understanding your budget, what money is coming in through your income, investments, rentals, and so on, and what you are spending is *key* to your other long-term goals.

Terms to Know

Run Rate: Your combined monthly and annual expenses
Fixed Costs: Costs that make up your fixed monthly expenses, such as rent/mortgage, utilities, groceries, and health care
Discretionary Spending: Costs that are more flexible such as entertainment, vacations, eating out, or nonessential purchases
Financial Goals Saving: Budgeted or automatic monthly savings for goals such as a down payment on a home, paying down debt, a large vacation, retirement, or education
Net Income: Your monthly/annual income after withholdings

Reflection

- How does your current financial run rate align with your long-term financial goals, and what adjustments can you make to ensure your spending and income are sustainable over time?

- Are you accurately tracking your run rate, and how does it reflect the sustainability of your finances over the long term? What changes might be needed to improve your financial health based on this analysis?

Finding Your Run Rate

Figuring out what you spend on fixed and discretionary expenses is a lot less fun than thinking about your goals or where to invest your money. However, there is a very important reason why this is the very first step: Until you understand what you are spending and where, it is impossible to truly do planning. Anything you plan for—a trip, retirement, education, paying off debt, buying a home—will be based on the resources you have saved and the income you can save monthly. Often, my clients think this is the toughest part of planning, so I have developed a simple way to measure annual spending. I do it this way because our monthly spending varies during the year with events, emergencies, and opportunities.

> Until you understand what you are spending and where, it is impossible to truly do planning.

DETERMINE YOUR MONTHLY AND ANNUAL RUN RATE

1. Pull together one year of statements from the account you use to pay your bills. Typically, this is a checking account at a bank or a credit union. It's important that it covers your credit card payments and cash payments such as Venmo and is where income is deposited. If you use multiple accounts, you will need a full year of statements from more than one account.

2. Circle the income on each statement (what came in—paychecks, social security, rent, interest, etc.) and what you spent (the total outflows). You may see some variance month to month with changing income and expenses.

3. Add up all your net (after-tax income) for the year and divide by twelve.

4. Add up all your expenses for the year and divide by twelve.

5. Subtract your monthly average expenses from your monthly average income.

When I do this exercise with clients, the first number (line 3) is usually higher than they told me it was originally. That's why I like to do budgeting this way. Sometimes we will look at two years to get a longer average. If you are guessing—trying to budget what you *think* you are spending—you will often forget the things that are not recurring expenses, such as holiday spending, travel, car repairs, and so on.

Once you understand your income sources, net monthly income, and expenses, you can start to dig into the numbers a bit. Determine where your discretionary and fixed expenses are going and whether they are in alignment with what makes you happy.

Further Reflections

- Do you know your cost of living—your run rate?

- Have you ever avoided looking at what it costs you to live for fear of being restricted?

- When you calculated your run rate, were you surprised by any of the numbers? Are you spending more than you thought?

- Are you spending money mindlessly in areas that do not bring you joy at the cost of more important goals?

Money Smarts

- The key to planning is understanding what it costs you to live monthly and annually.

- Understand what type of expenses you have—both discretionary and fixed costs.

- By establishing what you spend to live, you can more accurately plan for financial goals.

- Ignorance is not bliss! Freedom can be found in understanding your cost of living.

CHAPTER 8

Cash Reserves and Debt Management

Debt is like any other trap, easy enough to
get into, but hard enough to get out of.

—Henry Wheeler Shaw

One of the earliest conversations I remember having with my husband, Chris, about money involved debt. Chris and I met during our undergraduate studies and started our careers together. We both have always worked professionally with separate paychecks, and we chose to manage our money together. It's an easy decision when you are young and have nothing, but we both had our own memories and scars from our money experiences with our parents. Chris grew up in a family accustomed to living with credit card debt. He shared with me early on that credit card debt brought up deep, uncomfortable feelings from a childhood of being financially unstable.

When Chris and I had our premarital conversation about money, he said he would never criticize me for what I spent as long as we could pay off our credit cards every month and maintain some cash reserves. I committed to this, understanding his financial wounds, although I was not yet professionally working with people and their money. As of the writing of this book, we have been married for thirty-four years. Our credit cards have been paid monthly, and not once has Chris looked at a new pair of shoes on my feet and asked, "Oh, they are new? How much did they cost? Did you *need* a new pair of shoes?" We have worked together to achieve our financial goals, trying not to hit the old money wounds we both had from childhood. Money has been tight at times, but by keeping our credit cards as charge cards and paying them off monthly and having a cash reserve, conflict around money has not been an issue in our marriage.

Keeping money simple by reducing, eliminating, or never having high consumer debt levels and maintaining a cash reserve for unexpected moments is a beautiful way to live.

The Importance of a Cash Reserve

A cash reserve is the foundation of a strong financial life. When I find a lack of cash reserves and mounting debt, I know that client is spending beyond their means. It happens so easily, always thinking you will get caught up or make more money in the future. Then an emergency or opportunity arises, but you do not have a reserve, so you have to pass it up or it goes on a credit card with ridiculous interest, and you are in a debt spiral. Often this is accompanied by stress, sleepless nights, and staying in a job or a relationship that does not serve you because you have bills to pay. True financial freedom comes with choice. It's having enough money to cover those unexpected expenses or take an unexpected trip without going into credit card debt.

As of 2025, a significant portion of Americans are without an emergency fund. According to a Bankrate survey, 27 percent of US adults do not have an emergency fund, leaving them financially vulnerable in case of unexpected expenses.[1] Similarly, a report by LendingTree indicates that 49 percent of Americans could not cover a one thousand dollar emergency expense using only cash or funds from their checking or savings accounts.[2]

So, how much of a cash reserve should you have saved to build a life of financial security? It depends on several factors, such as how secure your job is, if there is a second income in the household, if you are a small business owner, or whether you have other assets you can use if needed. The rule of thumb most often used is three to six months of what you spend monthly (recall what you learned when you calculated your run rate).

> True financial freedom comes with choice.

Do you have a cash reserve and no revolving credit card debt at high rates? If you want to spend now but do not have money to fall back on and have to resort to using high-interest-rate credit cards in the hope that you will make more money in the future, you are setting yourself up for financial frustration. Your choices will be limited. But getting to the point that you pay your credit cards off in full and maintain a cash reserve is hard in the beginning—especially in a society that spends ahead of their earnings and is seemingly all over social media as a great lifestyle.

Our older daughter, Lauren, is in college. She is just learning what it takes to have a credit card, keep a cash reserve, and work. She is attending a university about a day's drive from our home. She loves to hike and visit national parks, so she took her car to college with her so she could continue her nature adventures.

But she needed her car at home during winter break, so I flew to her school and drove home with her.

The eight-hour car ride was a fantastic opportunity to catch up on her first semester of college and living independently. We talked about classes, social life, and what she looked forward to next semester. Lauren had always been excited to forge out on her own, and I was excited to hear about how she was handling the responsibility.

We were driving through beautiful mountains when Lauren took a deep breath and declared she wanted to be a nomad, saying the most challenging thing about "adulting" was having to think about money "all the time!" She was stressed by the whole process of earning money and then having to pay her credit card bills, worrying if what she was buying would put her over her limits or exhaust what she had in the bank.

"I want to live off the land, do odd jobs for money, and not worry," she declared. "I can go up one of those mountains and live."

Can you imagine being at the wheel when your daughter—who is at a university to further her education—declares she would prefer to be unhoused than to "worry about money all the time"? I was taken aback.

I looked over at her and said, "Okay—so, are you dropping out of college? That would save Daddy and me a lot of worry about money." We both started laughing so hard that I almost had to pull over and stop the car. Once we could breathe again, she confessed that she hadn't expected the pressure that came with having to manage her own money.

Lauren grew up in a home where we talked about money, and she has had to manage budgets since a young age—but at home, she had a full cupboard, laundry soap, shampoo, tooth-paste, and many other amenities she took for granted. When she had to buy them herself, she developed a whole new level of appreciation (and stress).

We are not the parents who sent our child to school with an unlimited credit card. To a large extent, the awareness of the "pressure" of money and the need to provide for her desires and needs was new. This first-semester learning was priceless, and home became a little more valued.

There are things we do in our lives that are so automatic we no longer think about them. Do you remember when you learned to tie your shoe or ride a bike? Once you get the hang of it, your brain develops a pattern for how to tie your shoe, and it becomes easy. You do it without even thinking about it. You likely also go on autopilot with your money; how you manage it moves from the conscious to a habit. Creating healthy habits around how we deal with the pressure of providing for our needs is key to our "money happiness."

As hard as it was for Lauren to be learning these lessons at nineteen, it allowed me to help her develop a healthy approach to thinking about money and managing it in a way that reduces stress. The key is keeping a cash reserve, paying off the credit cards monthly, and not getting behind.

Reflection

- How prepared are you to handle unexpected financial emergencies, and what would be the impact on your life if you didn't have a cash reserve?

- What are the potential risks of not having an emergency fund, and how might this affect your financial stability and peace of mind?

continued

> • How can building a cash reserve improve your financial confidence and help you avoid relying on debt during challenging times?

Establishing a Cash Reserve

How do you establish a cash reserve when you have credit card debt? In an ideal world, you have three to six months of cash reserve and no consumer credit card debt at high-interest rates. But if you are not there yet, how do you get there? Most people I talk to are not surprised by my recommendation not to carry consumer credit at high rates, but they have spent years and maybe generations using this very expensive way of financing things they want but do not have the money for. It takes time to change this pattern, but it is liberating when you do. Most people who carry a lot of debt and are trying to pay it down will take *all* their discretionary income and put as much as they can toward paying down their bills. However, if you do not build a cash reserve at the same time and you have an emergency, you are back to using credit cards, you are exhausted by not having any money, and you give up, thus staying in a never-ending cycle of high-interest debt.

HOW TO BREAK THE CREDIT CARD CYCLE

1. Line up your credit card bills and loans (student, personal loans, etc.) and create a list of what you owe and the interest you are paying. Determine what three months of cash reserves are

for you and what you have in discretionary income monthly. Each month take half of your discretionary income for credit card paydown and pay down your highest interest card balances first, while still paying the minimum on the others—protect your credit rating! Take the other half and start to build a cash reserve at the same time.

2. Get a second or third job until the high-interest credit cards are paid and your cash reserve is built.

3. Lower your fixed or nondiscretionary cost. Rent a less-expensive apartment, sell your car, eat out less, and so on. Typically, debt and the lack of a cash reserve result from overspending your income with fixed expenses that are higher than they should be for your income level.

None of these ideas are *fun*, but being debt-free is. Having money to fall back on and not drowning in credit card interest is liberating and will feel better than any object you buy. It will put you back in control of your financial future and success.

Further Reflections

- How are your cash reserves?
- How are you handling your consumer debt?
- What steps can you take to prioritize saving for an emergency fund, even if your current budget feels tight?

Money Smarts

- Keep money simple by reducing, eliminating, or never having high consumer debt levels and maintaining a cash reserve for unexpected moments.
- When you have a lack of cash reserves and mounting debt, that is a sign that your monthly spending may be beyond your means.
- Most people who carry a lot of debt and are trying to pay it down will take *all* their discretionary income and try to put as much as they can toward paying down their bills. This can create a debt loop; there is a better way.

CHAPTER 9

Protection Planning

The time to repair the roof
is when the sun is shining.

—John F. Kennedy

P rotection planning is a formal way to plan for catastrophic life events that could derail your financial plans and deplete your savings. I'm talking about insurance here. Let me begin by giving you my personal view: I absolutely dislike paying for insurance. But after all the years I have spent being involved with families and their money, I know that the things you do not think could happen to you will happen. And when they do, they can completely change the course of your financial life. Knowing your risk and then taking steps to protect your financial dreams is key.

Planning for the Certainty of Uncertainty

As a financial advisor in Washington, DC, I had the opportunity to work with many of the federal government agencies doing financial education. I had become a go-to expert on their pension plans and retirement. One of the human resource contacts I worked with was a man named Robert. He would have me come into a large meeting to present how to use the retirement benefit options that were offered to build a retirement plan. Robert and I became good friends. One day, after he had heard my presentation for the fortieth time (at least!), he asked me to meet with him to review his benefits and planning.

As we reviewed his goals for retirement, he shared with me that in his thirties, he had had cancer. He beat it and had been cancer-free now for more than ten years. Robert was forty-seven at the time of this discussion. He had not found a way to get life insurance and carried a very small amount through his government benefits. In doing Robert's planning, it was very clear to me that as the sole breadwinner in the family, if he was unable to work through retirement age to earn his full pension, the family would be in a financially compromised position for retirement.

Robert, my dear friend, loved to spend money. Saving was not his strong suit, but he had a great government pension if he could complete his years. His other goals were to pay for his girls' college educations and their potential future weddings. If he could continue to work, and if he lived to full retirement age, they would be in great shape. But if Robert were to die prematurely, it would greatly impact his family and their financial goals.

When I presented the financial plan I created to Robert and his wife, Carrie, I recommended a significant amount of life insurance for Robert—enough to ensure their desires for their girls and their retirement would be met. Robert hated insurance. He thought the premiums were a waste of money. I understood but still pushed. I encouraged Robert to go through underwriting to make sure he could get the coverage, given his medical history. I was thrilled when he was able to get coverage. Robert was not. He did not want to pay the premiums and refused the policy. We continued to work together, and every time we met, I pushed for life insurance, as I saw the lack of insurance as one of the greatest threats to their financial plans. Finally, he agreed to let me apply again, and once again he was approved. I delivered the policy, and again he did not want to sign it. Knowing the risks, I told him I was not leaving until he signed the policy. He did.

Four weeks went by without me hearing from him. This was unusual, and I thought I had really upset him by insisting he cover this risk. I called his office, and his assistant said, "Hi, Shannon. Robert is not here; he is at home today, so you may want to reach him there." I called his home, teased him for being home in the middle of the workday, and then asked him if he was upset with me since I hadn't heard from him. He asked me if I was sitting down, then proceeded to tell me that one week after I pushed him into accepting the life insurance policy, he'd had a massive heart attack. He told me that as he was being wheeled down the hospital hallway on a gurney, he'd stared at the lights on the ceiling, feeling grateful I had been such a "pushy financial advisor."

I laughed and said, "Well, you survived."

He got really quiet and replied, "Yes, the heart attack. But when they opened me up, they found the cancer is back. It is everywhere; I have fewer than six months to live."

Robert was forty-nine at this time. I was heartbroken.

I met with Robert and Carrie in their home to start the planning process for life without Robert. We built a plan to use his life insurance for the girls' education and, although Robert would not be able to walk his girls down the aisle, he would pay for their weddings. Carrie would be able to continue not working outside their home and be able to focus on the girls—all because of the life insurance policy.

Robert lived for eight more months. One week before he died, he called to thank me for giving him peace in his final days. My insistence for protection planning allowed him the comfort in his final days to know his family would be financially okay. I was twenty-nine, a new financial advisor. I learned very early in my career that life is uncertain, and protection planning is a key component of a financial plan. Protecting our financial risk and dreams is a cornerstone to financial planning.

> Life is uncertain, and protection planning is a key component of a financial plan.

A colleague of mine at my first firm would routinely say, "We need to plan for the certainty of uncertainty." Looking at your risk in the areas of health care, disability, life, and long-term care coverage is key to securing the financial future you desire for yourself and your family.

KEY AREAS OF RISK IN PERSONAL FINANCIAL PLANNING

Millions of Americans face substantial financial risks due to the lack of adequate insurance coverage. In 2024, over thirty million Americans remained without health insurance, one hundred million lacked life insurance, and many others were unprotected by disability insurance. This widespread coverage gap underscores the urgent need for policies that enhance the accessibility and affordability of these essential protections.[1] If you have the means to secure coverage for yourself and your loved ones, I highly advise you to pursue the following essential financial protections:

1. **Health insurance:** A contract that requires your health insurer to pay some or all of your health-care costs in exchange for a regular payment.

2. **Disability insurance:** A type of insurance that will provide income in the event you are unable to work due to disability.

3. **Life insurance:** Pays a lump sum known as a "death benefit" to your beneficiaries after your death.

4. **Long-term care insurance:** In the event you require ongoing care, this type of insurance reimburses you a daily amount (up to a preselected limit) for services to assist you with activities of daily living such as bathing, dressing, or eating.

Reflection

- How well does your current financial plan account for unexpected events, such as job loss, health emergencies, or major life changes?

- Are you adequately insured to protect yourself and your family from financial setbacks, and what areas of your insurance coverage might need attention?

Understanding Your Risk

Do you always have to buy insurance to cover these needs? Absolutely not! But understanding your personal risk and the resources you have—or don't have—to meet your health, disability, death, and long-term-care needs is how you start to evaluate.

What is the easiest way to decide? Run the numbers. In planning, we look at what would happen to the family or an individual's financial goals if they experienced one of these risks. Let me give you an example: If you earn $75k a year and are disabled by an accident or an illness and unable to work, would your disability insurance cover your expenses? Would you still be able to save for financial goals? What if you were unable to work for years? Do you have enough resources or insurance to meet your expenses and financial goals?

This process of running the numbers on these situations that you hope will never happen is hard. In fact, many people are superstitious when it comes to even talking about the potential for premature death, disability, or long-term care. They're afraid that if they even think about these things, they will be more likely to happen. These topics may be difficult for you to review and run the numbers, but they can be catastrophic to your overall financial goals if left unconsidered. Taking time to review your risk, create a plan, or insure against the risk could profoundly impact your financial goals if you are faced with one of these catastrophic life events.

Further Reflections

- Have you considered running different financial scenarios to understand how your plan would hold up under various risks, such as market downturns, job loss, or unexpected expenses?

- What potential risks are you overlooking in your financial planning, and how can scenario analysis help you identify and prepare for these risks?

Money Smarts

- Plan for the certainty of uncertainty.

- Protection planning is a formal way to plan for catastrophic life events that could derail your financial plans and deplete your savings.

- Protecting your risk in the areas of health care, disability, life, and long-term-care coverage may be vital to securing the financial future you desire for yourself and your family.

CHAPTER 10

Putting Your Money to Work

Investing isn't about beating others at their game.
It's about controlling yourself at your own game.

—Jason Zweig

L et me be clear: I did not set out to write a book on invest-ing. There are thousands on the market, and people still fall short of their money desires every day. However, it would be remiss of me not to offer you a basic understanding of investing as part of building your financial foundation. Just remember: Investing is not the endgame. You may be drawn to others—professionals or influencers—who know how to talk about investing. You may want to know what will happen next in the "markets" so you can get ahead and strike it rich—or at least make enough money not to have to think about money again! You can buy books, listen to motivational speakers, and ask friends about the "returns" they get from their brokers. You might spend valuable time seeking "hot tips" because you feel you are missing the golden nugget of information that will help you reach all of your goals—preferably overnight, please!

A significant number of people find investing challenging or confusing. According to a Fidelity study, more than half of teens consider investing too confusing, indicating a need for better financial education early on.[1] This sentiment is echoed in the broader population as well. For instance, a survey by Citizens Bank found that nearly three-quarters of Americans (72 percent) lack the financial confidence needed to manage a large influx of money on their own. This indicates a widespread struggle with understanding complex financial concepts, including investment strategies.[2]

Historically, wealth is built by investing over time, with your short-term needs liquid and your long-term money invested according to the risk tolerance you can handle when it declines. Boring! Yep, robust investment plans usually are. But you may have been given a different idea from the many movies made about Wall Street, which have skewed what nearly everyone thinks they need to know or do with their money.

> Investing is not the endgame.

Know Your Investment Risk Tolerance

When I start working with a new investor, and we discuss risk, I will often begin by saying, "We are getting on a roller coaster together. I will be strapped in with you. If you get concerned or throw up on my shoes, no problem. If you jump out, we have a bigger issue." When you align your risk and get invested, there will be nervous moments and potentially a year or two of negative performance; if you are invested in alignment with your risk tolerance, you may throw up emotionally, get scared, lose some sleep, and so on. But if you jump out of the markets, you may do long-term damage to your investing goals.

Getting your risk aligned correctly is one of the most challenging investing tasks. It is especially tough when equity markets have been on an upward trend. Everyone is at higher risk then! Let it roll! But when the markets are falling, there is a significant emotional toll, and if you are not clear on why you are investing and the risk you are taking for your goals, you could create considerable damage to your long-term investment goals by pulling out of the markets at that time. And it's so easy to do when you have days, weeks, months, or years of negative returns. Boring wins the day in investing with respect to your risk tolerance. It may seem more "fun" or "educated" to take risks you are uncomfortable with, but it is not a good long-term strategy.

Reflection

- How comfortable are you with the possibility of losing money in your investments, and how does this align with your current investment strategy?

- Have you accurately assessed your risk tolerance, and how might your emotional responses to market volatility affect your long-term investment decisions?

- How would you respond to a significant market downturn, and do you have a strategy in place to manage your investments during times of uncertainty?

Investing 101

Investing can be a powerful way to grow your wealth because stocks historically have provided significant returns over long periods. If you had a savings account of $10,000 that earned 1 percent a year, in twenty years you would have $12,202. If you invested $10,000 in the S&P Index fund for twenty years at a conservative estimated rate, based on historical returns of 8 percent, you would have $45,610. Of course, investments go up and down in the real world, so there is never a consistent return every year. But in the long run, historically speaking, investing has far outpaced keeping your money in a savings account or under your mattress.

HOW INVESTING WORKS

When investing, you hope to grow your wealth over time by purchasing financial assets such as stocks, bonds, or exchange-traded funds (ETFs) to generate returns. Investing works by buying financial assets that have the potential to grow in value while managing risk in alignment with your goals and time horizon. Investing includes more than simply the stock market. It can mean putting your money into bonds, real estate, currency, collectibles, fine art, and more.

FOUR MAIN ASSET CLASSES

Asset classes are categories of investments. There are many types of asset classes, but these are the main four you will come across:

1. **Stocks:** When you buy a stock, you become a partial company owner. You earn money if the stock (the company) becomes

more valuable. This usually happens when the company increases profit. Some stocks will also pay dividends—a small profit that is distributed as cash or shares to the owners (stockholders).

2. **Bonds:** A bond is a loan to the entity that is selling the bond. They are most often companies or governments. The bond will pay a stated interest rate for a set amount of time, and usually you receive your entire initial investment back when the bond matures (the term is up).

3. **Cash:** This is what you have in your wallet, a savings, or checking account. There are other types of cash, such as money market accounts. Cash earns interest, usually much lower than a bond, and is generally considered safe. However, sometimes it is not safe, and you need to understand the risks of the cash vehicle you are in.

4. **Alternative Investments:** These are considered more risky investments and do not fit the first three asset classes. They include real estate, private equity, cryptocurrencies, commodities such as gold, and many more.

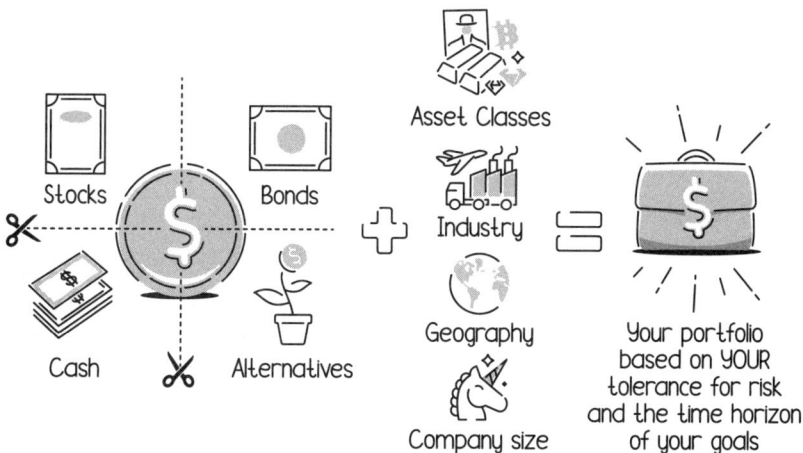

Stocks

Bonds

Cash

Alternatives

Asset Classes

Industry

Geography

Company size

Your portfolio based on YOUR tolerance for risk and the time horizon of your goals

DIVERSIFICATION AND ASSET ALLOCATION

Diversification is dividing your assets into different asset classes to minimize risk. You are spreading out the risk. It can be spread out not only into other asset classes but also different parts of the world, types of companies, and company sizes. If you have heard the old saying "Don't put all your eggs in one basket," that is essentially what diversification is. Remember the story of Gary and Sue who invested everything in the technology sector?

Investors frequently believe they can predict market movements or rely on forecasts. However, academic research indicates that market predictions are generally unreliable, and it's more effective to focus on long-term trends and diversified portfolios rather than short-term market timing.[3]

When using asset allocation, you should consider your time horizon, how long until you need the money, how comfortable you are with risk, and the volatility of the investment. An example of asset allocation would be putting a percentage of your investments in stocks and bonds.

I am outlining basic concepts here so you can understand the language of investing. Finding the proper allocation for your investments is a critical part of investing. If you invest, you will have years when your portfolio (basket of assets) loses money. What will you do? If you pull your money out because of fear, you may lose more than if you kept the money in a safe investment, such as cash. So why do people invest? Because historically, over time, investing creates returns that are worth the risk. But not all risks are the same. Some investments do become worthless and you lose all your money. Creating a plan by working with an advisor or a trusted friend or family member who can guide and educate you is critical. You can also take classes on investing. The key is to educate yourself on the risks and the different types of vehicles that are available.

Further Reflections

- What is your experience with investing?

- Do you understand your risk tolerance?

- How does your risk tolerance change based on different stages of your life or financial goals, and are you adjusting your portfolio accordingly?

Money Smarts

- Wealth is typically built by investing over time, with your short-term needs liquid and your long-term money invested in the risk tolerance you can handle when markets decline.

- Investing involves buying financial assets that have the potential to grow in value while managing risk in alignment with your goals and time horizon.

- Diversification is dividing your assets into different asset classes to minimize risk.

- The key is to educate yourself on the risks and the different types of vehicles that are available.

- **WARNING:** There are many types of investments, and they all carry various levels of risk. Always know what you are investing in, why you are investing in a particular vehicle, and what the historical returns are. This falls under the adage "There are no dumb questions." If someone is making you feel that way, *run*! Do *not* invest with them.

CHAPTER 11

What Is Your Money Legacy?

The key to leaving a lasting legacy is intentionality. By planning your estate, you ensure that what you worked hard for benefits those you love and care about.

—Dave Ramsey

When it comes to money, legacy can have a lot of different meanings. To most, it is encapsulated in one word: inheritance. The old saying "You can't take it with you" is a reminder that money is something you interact with only while you're alive. When you think about leaving money for your heirs, you probably envision helping the next generation or a charity with deep meaning to you. But what really happens after you die? When your money is passed to the next generation or to a charity, they can use it as they wish unless you have a well-defined trust specifying how it should be allocated.

The money you leave represents the financial part of your legacy—your life's work. If family values are misaligned around money in life, after a death it could even get worse. There is *some* level of dysfunction in every family I have ever worked with. If proper planning is not done, estates can be caught up for years in the legal system. What can be even more concerning is that when values around money were not taught, decades, if not generations, of money can be spent as quickly as lottery winnings. When you think about your estate—the assets and the values you leave—how does it reflect your life, your legacy?

Crafting an Enduring Legacy

Rebecca and Randy sat across from me in my office. They were both professors of science at a major university and also worked for a small lab researching cancer through grants. They were the leading experts in their field, and after decades, they were still inspired by their work. As they grew closer to retirement, they continued to shepherd young PhD candidates into their field of study and publish their own legacy of work for students to learn from in the future. When Randy's mother passed, he inherited several million dollars. They wanted to discuss how to handle the new inheritance without any apparent heirs. They explained to me that beyond wanting to travel extensively, they had everything they wanted.

When exploring options, I asked them, "If you could create a legacy that endures after you both have passed, what would that be?" Without hesitation, they told me they had been so grateful for all the donations made to their lab that supported their research that they wanted to be the donors now, so their life's research work would be funded and able to continue. We worked through many different options on how to give some of the inheritance they had received to create an endowment for research. Ultimately, with good health, they purchased a second-to-die life insurance policy. This type of life insurance does not pay out a benefit at the first death but instead pays at the second death. They only wanted to use a portion of Randy's inheritance. We were able to secure a multi-million-dollar policy that would be paid as a grant to continue their research. In doing so, they created a legacy of money in alignment with their deepest values. Every year when we meet, they continue to thank me for the strategy that has brought them so much joy.

Reflection

- What values and principles do you want your financial legacy to reflect, and how can you ensure that your money aligns with those values?

- How can you balance enjoying your wealth in the present while still building a lasting financial legacy for others?

No Estate Plan Creates Chaos

Kate called my office on a cool November afternoon. She had been referred to me by a mutual friend. She quietly wept as she told me that she had lost her husband, Steve, a year earlier to a heart attack. She told me he'd had a substantial life insurance policy; the death benefit had been paid out, but she couldn't bring herself to look at the money because it meant he really was gone. The money was sitting in her checking account, and she knew she needed to use the insurance proceeds to build a plan for herself and her kids. Kate had never worked outside of the home, and she felt vulnerable, as Steve had handled all the finances.

When Kate and I met in my office, we created a financial plan with an investment structure to generate income for her and the kids to replace the lost income from Steve. We also discussed how important it was, especially now, for Kate to create an estate plan in case something happened to her, because she was the only surviving parent of two minor children. I put her in touch with a few estate planning attorneys. It was clear that Kate was distraught over the loss of Steve, but she understood she needed to get her legacy in order, as the children were young and still in school.

A few weeks later, Kate and I met to review her investments and income. I asked her how the progress was going with the estate planning attorney. She said she just could not bring herself to start the process; thinking about her own death so close to her husband's was emotional, but she understood the risk it posed to her children if something should happen to her. She also confided that she found the process complicated and intimidating. I offered to go with her to meet the estate planning attorney as a way to help this very important step along.

Three months after this last meeting, Kate's sister called my office. It was one of those calls you pray you never receive—there had been an accident, and Kate had been killed. Gratefully, the kids had been at school and not in the car. It had been a multicar accident on the highway that I would see later on the evening news. Although I had been very persistent, in her grief, Kate had not created an estate plan or dealt with the final financial details of Steve's estate.

The following two years were a nightmare of work for Kate's sister. It started with the basic needs of dealing with the smashed-up car, the insurance, the burial, and custodianship of the two children. I know Kate and Steve loved their children dearly, and Kate was very close to her sister; she had never intended to create such a time-consuming mess in the midst of her sister's grief. Kate's legacy of not addressing estate planning basics created years of work, disappointment, and stress for her family as well as fights around custodianship of the children and the money.

According to Caring.com's 2024 wills survey, 40 percent of Americans don't think they have enough assets to create a will. Accordingly, approximately 55 percent of Americans die without a will or estate plan, according to various surveys and studies. As we've seen with Kate and Steve, this lack of estate planning can lead to significant issues for surviving family members, including lengthy and costly probate processes, potential family conflicts, and the distribution of assets in ways that might not align with the deceased's wishes.[1]

Often, estate planning is one of those items I find people pushing off until "tomorrow." Discussing our mortality can be difficult, and some are superstitious that in doing so, we can invite tragedy. I encourage you to see how *not* doing so creates a problematic legacy for those you love the most.

Reflection

- How do you want to be remembered by future generations, and what financial steps can you take today to build that legacy?

continued

- What fears or uncertainties might be holding you back from creating an estate plan, and how can you address these to ensure your loved ones are protected and your wishes are fulfilled?

Leaving Your Legacy Is a Family Affair

In addition to your estate itself, you also leave a legacy of your values around money. Often, we hear stories of people inheriting money their families worked hard for and blowing it all in a few years. I can tell you that the stories are real. Money given to heirs without clear values is often blown quickly. I live in the United States, and we still have difficulty discussing money with our families. We need to get over this! We are creating a shroud of secrecy that prevents a healthy money legacy.

Imagine if your parents sat down with you before passing and told you what they owned, how they earned their money, what they did to save it, and their values around money. Would it change how you handled your inheritance from them? Well, in my experience, it does.

One of the things I love about my profession is that I get to sit with real people every day. One of the meetings I offer to do with my clients is a family meeting, and it is one of the most powerful meetings we do. We bring in the whole family—the parents *and* the heirs. We prepare the parents on how to disclose the assets and how they earned, invested, and spent them. They also discuss what they hope their heirs will do with the money. Talk about passing down values and respect for their hard-earned money! Of course, families come in many forms, but the key is having the heirs in the room with the people who will be leaving them money.

What is magical about this process is it makes the issue of money transparent within the family. No one is left wondering if they are being left money or assets. The heirs can also learn about what is hoped for them and the money. This can create an understanding of how decisions were made directly from their families or friends versus the mystery "will reading" scene in movies that always seems to kick off a major family feud! To avoid imbuing your personal legacy with that kind of drama, transparency is critical to create a healthy environment for wealth transfer.

Reflection

- Have you created a clear and comprehensive estate plan that will preserve and distribute your wealth according to your wishes?
- What conversations should you be having with your family or loved ones to ensure your financial legacy is carried forward in the way you intend?

Estate Planning Basics

Estate planning covers the transfer of assets after a person dies. How is this different from just having a will? Simply put, estate planning is a broader plan for where your assets will go after you die, who will be the guardians of your children, and more. The main goal of estate planning is to protect your loved ones. I often refer to it as your last love letter to your family. If you do not plan, your estate can fall into probate, the court-supervised legal process of distributing your assets in the United States. It can be very long and expensive, and your assets most likely will not go to the people or organizations you intended. Estate planning can also help you make medical or financial decisions if you cannot due to an accident, memory loss, illness, and so on.

> The main goal of estate planning is to protect your loved ones. It is your last love letter to your family.

In the United States and other parts of the world, you can make a beneficiary designation that allows you to directly transfer an asset, regardless of the terms of your will. These are often made on financial accounts, retirement accounts, and life insurance policies. *Be aware*: These need to be reviewed often. Beneficiary designations will override a will and a trust (if the designation is not to the trust). If you have had a life transition, such as a marriage, divorce, death, or a falling out with another person, you may want to check all your beneficiary designations.

I am not an estate planning attorney, but I encourage all my clients to work with one. An estate planning attorney can walk you through all the nuances of the essential planning documents to consider, which include:

- Wills and trusts
- Durable power of attorney
- Medical or health care power of attorney
- Living wills and advance directives for medical decisions

Further Reflections

- Have you clearly outlined your wishes for the distribution of your assets, and do you fully understand the legal tools available, such as wills, trusts, and powers of attorney?

- How often are you reviewing and updating your estate plan to ensure it reflects your current financial situation, family dynamics, and personal goals?

- Have you adequately considered tax implications in your estate planning, and how you can structure your plan to minimize taxes for your heirs?

Money Smarts

- Your financial legacy is how you leave your money when you die.

- Estate planning is essential for leaving a healthy money legacy.

- Estate planning is not just for distribution of assets after death. It can also address how medical and financial decisions are made for you when you are unable to do so.

- Please consider working with an estate planning attorney to review your current document or create new documents in alignment with your values.

CHAPTER 12

Habits and Resilience

Often, people tell me that it is hard to
create new habits that involve how they think
about money and interact with it. But let me
assure you it is much harder if you do not.

—Mel Robbins

A habit is an acquired repeatable behavior that has become nearly or completely involuntary. You likely do many things without thinking; you are simply reacting or repeating what you have always done. How you interact and think about your money is often so deeply entrenched in your habits that it is hard to change your thoughts and behaviors.

In my 2021 TEDx Talk,[1] I spoke about my retired clients Joe and Wendy. They save enough to meet their retirement income needs but are uncomfortable spending money. They have grandchildren on the East Coast but are afraid to spend money on airline tickets. They are always waiting for something to compromise their financial security. Would it surprise you to learn that Joe's parents lost everything in the Great Depression, and he grew up always preparing for the next economic disaster? I understood that if I was going to help them with their dreams of seeing their grandchildren, I had to help them break their habitual thinking with hard evidence that they had the resources to make the flight to the East Coast a couple of times a year without jeopardizing their financial security. I modeled their portfolio to reflect a decline in the S&P 500 of 38.49 percent. I chose that percentage because of the S&P 500 drop during the Great Recession in 2008. Even if we should experience another deep decline in the markets like that, Joe and Wendy will still have enough resources to purchase two round-trip airline tickets a year. Joe continues to worry about running out of money and probably always will, but now they visit their grandchildren. Joe and Wendy needed to create a new habit of thinking about spending money.

For those who spend too much and have gotten into the habit of an endless debt cycle, the story of Joe and Wendy sounds crazy, but there are different types of limiting habits. Sometimes, a habit that feels justified, such as saving and not spending, can also become a limiting habit where resources are not enjoyed.

Living with Limiting Habits

Christine was a successful human resource professional, earning at a level that allowed her to live independently and save for retirement. Although she had a career that supported her life-style and goals, her habits jeopardized her dreams. Christine had been single for some time, and she enjoyed dating. When the relationships became serious, she often allowed her boyfriend to move into her home with her. The habitual pattern that started to emerge was the men she was choosing all needed financial support. The final boyfriend-roommate, who helped her identify this emotional habit, moved into her home and asked her to fund his start-up business.

This man, let's call him James, worked as a fast-food restaurant manager but dreamed of opening a consulting company. He convinced Christine to fund the business, although he had no entrepreneurial experience. When Christine and I met, she asked me to liquidate a large portion of her retirement funds to invest in James's business idea. We discussed at length the tax implications of withdrawing the money in a lump sum and risking her hard-earned retirement money for what appeared to be a very high-risk investment. Christine was resolute and withdrew the money.

A little more than six months later, Christine called my office in tears. She had just met with the CPA and had a large tax bill due. The business funding that had been taken from Christine's IRA withdrawal had resulted in a hefty tax bill. She told me the consulting company was not producing revenue, and she realized that James could not run the business. She had invested most of her retirement savings, and it was gone. Despite how resolute she had been when she asked me for the money, she now felt foolish for trusting James and investing her hard-earned money.

This was a habitual pattern she had developed regarding her dating life. She told me on that call that her father had been abusive to her growing up. She said the physical and mental abuse she grew up with made her feel like she had to earn love, which led to her choosing men who needed her financially. She went on to let me know that she was seeking professional counseling to try to break this habitual cycle that was destroying her financial goals.

Habits around money can come in many forms. Many are

> Habits around money can come in many forms. Many are deeply engrained, and we may not even recognize the pattern of behavior as a recurring habit influencing our financial dreams.

deeply engrained, and we may not even recognize the pattern of behavior as a recurring habit influencing our financial dreams. With Christine, it took a large tax bill and the loss of decades of retirement savings to recognize the damage her habit of choosing financially needy men was creating in her financial life.

Old Habits Die Hard

Several factors influence the difficulty of forming new habits. Both the new behavior's complexity and the individual's environment play significant roles. Simple habits, such as drinking water with lunch, become automatic faster than more complex ones, such as daily exercise routines or detailed financial management strategies.[2]

For example, we all live in a society with information at our disposal. If you feel lacking in an area, such as money management, you can simply google "how to manage money" or "how to make better financial decisions." You likely often find suggestions for getting things done in new and improved ways—maybe even YouTube videos demonstrating this. So why is it so easy to slip back into old ways and never make a change?

Creating a new habit around anything is difficult. Looking closely at your life, you will see that you have small daily habits you are not conscious of most of the time. Without this kind of autopilot, you would spend the whole day having to overthink everything you do! Unexamined habits govern and limit what you can experience. They can keep goals always out of reach.

Poor financial habits can lead to financial struggles and stress both today and in the future. Problems with money can also lead to high levels of mental disorders around money, personal relationships, loss of dreams, and even homelessness. Here are a few examples I have witnessed firsthand:

- **Problem habit:** Working past the point of retiring out of fear of not having enough money, then ending up with a disabling illness and, despite having ample financial resources, never being able to take part in the dream of traveling during retirement.

  - **New habit:** Cultivating the discipline to do annual planning.

- **Problem habit:** Never establishing a budget, spending on things that do not bring happiness, and missing out on important financial goals.

  - **New habit:** Annual review of the expenditure, savings, and goals. Time is one of the most significant multipliers. The sooner you establish goals, what they will cost, and the money you have to save from your budget, the greater your chance of meeting your goals, such as retirement.

- **Problem habit:** Not establishing an adequate cash reserve and living on expensive credit card debt.

  - **New habit:** Getting a handle on spending, controlling debt ratios, having a cash reserve, and having money to meet emergencies or opportunities. This habit is worth the pain, as the pain of regret on this is high.

These are just a few examples of how habits play a crucial role in financial success by instilling discipline, reducing decision fatigue, and fostering long-term economic stability.

Reflection

- Are you prioritizing short-term wants over long-term financial security, and how can you shift your habits to build a healthier financial foundation?

- What emotions or beliefs influence your money habits at home, and how can you become more mindful of these behaviors to improve your financial success?

The Role of Resilience

How do you build new habits? Through resilience. The American Psychological Association defines resilience as "the process and outcome of successfully adapting to difficult or challenging life experiences, especially through mental, emotional, and behavioral flexibility and adjustment to external and internal demands."[3]

I love the word *resilience* because it has the potential to make us feel strong and gives us hope when we tap into it. However, often we do a great job until there is a crisis, and then resilience fades. You likely want to see grit and resilience as part of your character. Self-made stories, rags-to-riches stories, and survival stories are inspiring. The entertainment industry uses this desire for triumph over flawed habits by producing inspiring stories where the underdog wins, creating feel-good moments within a short journey of a movie or TV show. The experience likely leaves you with the drive to do things differently for yourself. Yet you likely find you cannot bounce back as quickly as your favorite movie heroes.

Regarding money, resilience and habit-building are even more difficult. Thinking about finances can produce a broad band of fear-based emotions. You may still hear the voices of others in your life as well as your own negative thoughts and feelings. By aligning your values with your money, you can build better habits and grow your resilience to stick to your goals. When you know why you are saving, budgeting, and investing, you understand the why behind the habits, and your resilience grows. You can choose *not* to act on them. By not acting on them, you can create lasting change in your life—new pathways.

Christine created a new pathway of choosing a partner who would not drain her financially. It took resilience for her to walk away from James. She had to do a lot of rebuilding to meet her retirement goals, but eventually Christine found love and is happily married to a partner who can contribute financially to their

CUE

HABITS

Making one
positive
change

REWARD

ROUTINE

retirement. Today, she is the living embodiment of the fact that resilient individuals are better equipped to make sound financial decisions under pressure. They can manage emotions such as fear and anxiety, which often lead to poor financial choices. According to a report by the Consumer Financial Protection Bureau, resilience is linked to better financial decision-making and overall financial well-being.[4] Dealing with money will always be emotional. And because it is emotional, developing resilience and understanding how you feel, think, and interact with money is the golden key to true financial success.

How to Build Financial Resilience

- Have a plan: You need a clear vision of what is important to you to make the best financial decisions in times of change.

- Even if you are thrown off your plan, you'll know where to start again when you are back on track.

- Have a cash reserve and pay off consumer debt.

- Know your cost of living.

- Protect your potential risks.

- When you have a financial question or issue, use it as an opportunity to build your financial knowledge and resources.

- Seek professionals in taxation, investments, insurance, financial planning, and banking. Line up your team and ask many questions. If you do not understand, ask again.

- Recognize your emotional and financial history and determine if it impacts your financial habits today.

Further Reflections

- What money habits are impacting your financial life? Can you identify their positive or negative impact on your goals?

- Do you regularly review and adjust financial goals to ensure they stay aligned with your evolving life circumstances and priorities?

- What small, consistent actions can you take to build resilient financial habits, such as automatic savings or cutting unnecessary expenses?

- Are you educating yourself on financial matters regularly, and how does ongoing learning contribute to your financial resilience?

Money Smarts

- How you interact and think about your money is often so deeply entrenched in your habits that it is hard to change your thoughts and behaviors.

- Money is emotional. Developing resilience and understanding how you feel, think, and interact with money is the golden key to true financial success.

CHAPTER 13

Confidence and Course Corrections

Don't wait until everything is just right. It will
never be perfect. There will always be challenges,
obstacles, and less-than-perfect conditions. So
what? Get started now. With each step you take,
you will grow stronger and stronger, more and
more skilled, more and more self-confident,
and more and more successful.

—Mark Victor Hansen

A sense of confidence and agency is critical when you set
out to create the financial life you want. If you do not feel
you have control, you become a victim of your money—
and believe me, it's easy to let that happen with all the financial
wounds we carry.

The loss of a job, an unexpected illness, debt cycles, and a lack
of knowledge about how to work with money are all able to create
financial wounds that rob you of your confidence. Day-to-day life
can take its toll, too. You can be so busy trying to earn money to
meet your needs, raise your kids, and take care of aging parents
that you do not have the time to focus on your long-term goals.

Having confidence in your goals can be tricky. This is because you have grown comfortable with your own stories about why you are not creating or achieving your financial goals. You have dug deep neural pathways in your brain to respond in specific ways and thought patterns. When I was first working in finance, someone told me, "Fake it until you make it." What they essentially were saying was, "If you do not have the confidence to do what you need to do, act like you do and the confidence will come." I found this problematic because I did not want to *fake* my knowledge. However, what I did do was create a habit of just continuing forward and taking the next step by asking a lot of questions. (The expression *just keep swimming* from the movie *Finding Nemo* is always in my mind.) By doing this, I created absolute confidence in myself that I would learn my job well. And I did.

So often, negative self-talk, or what people refer to as "feeling like an imposter," gets in the way of taking that next step, researching the necessary knowledge, or asking "dumb" questions. My first-grade English teacher, Mrs. Sorensen, would say, "There are no dumb questions—only the ones that are not asked." And she was right. Once you get transparent about what you tell yourself about money, you will recognize the negative thought-loops faster. This can significantly impact your confidence as you align your money management with your dreams and desires.

Expertise Only Goes So Far

Financial confidence among people varies widely. According to a 2023 survey by Unbiased, only 25 percent of adults in the United States consider themselves extremely confident about their finances, while 17 percent reported no financial confidence at all.

Additionally, 10 percent said they are not confident in any area of finance.[1] Overall, financial confidence is low, with many individuals struggling to understand financial terms and feeling intimidated to seek professional financial advice.[2] I have seen these statistics reflected in my work. Over the years, I have had countless opportunities to meet with people who are experts in their fields, and they have come to me to help them manage their money. Many of them, despite their financial success and enormous professional expertise, found their progress toward financial goals impeded by low confidence.

One of my early career experiences especially taught me a lot about money confidence. I was working in Washington, DC, at the time and had an initial meeting with a CEO who had been referred to me. My own confidence was shaky as I went downtown to meet with this very powerful man. What was running through my head was, *What can I help a CEO with? He must know a lot more about money than I do.* I was intimidated by my respect for his success in his business. But, as I have done many times before, I walked into the meeting ready to ask questions and help where I could. That day, Jack, the CEO, gave me one of the greatest gifts of my career and helped me gain confidence in my role.

Jack's assistant showed me to his office and told me he would be in shortly and that his wife, Kay, was running a few minutes behind but would also join us. As I sat down at the table, Jack entered and closed the door slowly behind him. In almost a whisper, he thanked me for coming to his office and said he wanted to talk with me privately before his wife arrived. He went on to tell me that as successful as he had been in building his business, he had not had time to really learn how to create a financial plan or invest. He said he was unsure about very basic financial products and how they worked for retirement planning. His wife assumed that he had been handling the investing and had left it all up to him. He was worried he would be found out that day in the meeting and hoped that I could help him through the process of learning without losing the confidence of his wife. I assured him I would.

Jack, Kay, and I have had some good laughs about that day over the years. Jack came clean with Kay about his lack of knowledge about investing, and it turned out that Kay wanted to take the lead in their financial planning while Jack ran the business. Today, they are comfortably retired, and Kay still enjoys being involved in the "money" side of their planning more than Jack.

If you are an expert in one field, you may find that you expect yourself to be an expert with your money, too. But even if you are successful in earning money, that does not necessarily correlate with investment and financial planning knowledge. Jack found his confidence that day in taking a risk and being vulnerable. I, too, gained confidence that day in my approach to money conversations. It was a beautiful reminder that we all carry emotion around money, even a successful CEO.

Identifying Negative Money Thoughts

Do you have negative thoughts that keep you from having money confidence? Here are a few I have heard, but I'm sure you can add to my list:

- It's all too complicated. I feel dumb asking questions I should know the answers to.

- I'm so busy that I don't have time to focus on this right now. I will do it another time.

- I will never earn enough to really achieve what I want financially, so why set goals?
- My parents never talked about money; it is rude to do so.
- I made some bad investments; I am just not good with money.
- We should have started years ago, but now it's just too late.
- It's depressing to think about.

Reflection

- What areas of your financial life make you feel uncertain, and how can you gain more knowledge or support to build your confidence?
- How can you track your financial progress to reinforce positive habits and strengthen your belief in your ability to manage money effectively?
- What small financial wins have you already achieved, and how can you build on them to boost your confidence in managing larger financial goals?

Expect Course Corrections!

You have figured out what you want for yourself. You've created a clear plan, been transparent about your money talk tracks, and are confident that you can reach your goals in time. But what if something changes? And it always does. You set yourself up when you expect perfection. Chris and I often tell our girls, "There are no perfect people, and we will not be the first."

How you handle your failures and setbacks is what really matters. When you fail, you have an opportunity to learn. How will you respond when you have a financial setback? Your response is what really matters. Do you become stagnant? Do you wallow in your disappointment or shame, or do you learn that what you tried did not work? Then try again and again. If you do not expect setbacks, you then have a much higher chance of getting into a victim loop. If you are a victim of your financial life or thoughts, it will be much harder to change your habits.

Life does not happen in straight lines. Things change, and you must make financial decisions every day throughout these changes. These changes to your financial life will not always be harmful, but they can be disruptive. Knowing what you want for yourself gives you an internal compass or north star that can help you course-correct during times of change.

Let me give you a personal example. When my husband and I were in our early thirties, our core financial goals included travel, buying a larger home, and saving for retirement. We had a dream vacation planned to Africa—the most expensive trip ever—but then my husband went through an unexpected job transition. We asked ourselves, "Do we take the trip?"

Our first thought was to cancel the trip, save the money, and buckle down financially until Chris landed a new job. It seemed like the responsible thing to do. How could we enjoy the trip with this uncertainty hanging over us? The easy decision would have been to cancel, but instead we went on the trip. Travel was one of our core financial values. Decades later, we still remember that trip. We met Barbara and Mark on that trip, and they remain some of our closest friends to this day. We used our resources in alignment with our values. We did not allow the financial uncertainty of a job transition to change our plans. But we did have to make a course correction. When we returned, we had to use some of our cash reserves to pay the credit card bill for the trip. Over the next six months, we were cautious about eating at home more than dining out, and we curbed our spending on other things to make sure we rebuilt our cash reserve.

So often bumps in the road will throw you off the course of your financial goals. Expect bumps and decide how you will respond. Going on a trip during a job transition may not seem like a big deal, but when you are afraid financially, you may find that you stop spending until you are comfortable again. I have seen people live in fear for decades, never spending on

> Expect bumps and decide how you will respond.

what would really make them happy. It almost seems as if they are punishing themselves for changes that were out of their control.

The more productive response is to make course corrections to your original plan in light of the new situation. Your goals must adapt to life's twists and turns, so learn to correct the course. If a road is closed, the navigational service you use to map your drive reroutes you, and there may be several different roads you can take to carry you forward to your destination. In my example, we changed our spending on things that were not as important to us to make sure we could take a trip, which was one of our core goals.

Thousands of things can throw off a financial plan or goal: job loss, illness, market volatility, unexpected expenses, a new baby, planning for an exciting opportunity on the horizon or a change in income, to name a few. One of the big bumps in the road of the last couple of decades was the Global Financial Crisis of 2008. I still hear people blame their current financial situation on the loss they experienced almost fifteen years ago. They were so thrown by the pullback in the markets or the loss of a home that they were unable to rebuild their financial dreams. They talk about wanting to start again, but fear has them frozen.

With clear financial goals, you know where you want to go, and you can learn to adjust. You might need to save more, give a plan more time, or sacrifice another goal to stay on track. There usually are many routes to choose from financially. You do not need to lose sight of your long-term financial dreams due to a short-term change. Course-correct and just keep swimming.

Reflection

- How do you typically respond to financial challenges, and what can you learn from past setbacks to improve your ability to recover and adapt?

- What specific steps can you take to course-correct after a financial setback, and how can you ensure these actions align with your long-term goals?

- Are you giving yourself enough time and space to reflect on what caused the setback, and how can you use this insight to avoid similar issues in the future?

Identify the Need for Course Correction

Do you need to make some course corrections in your financial life? Have you ever had thoughts like the following?

- I want, desire, or am inspired when I think of having *it* (insert your dream), but I procrastinate or am unwilling to do the work.

- I do not set time aside for my dreams: the to-dos, the footwork, the putting pen to paper.

- There is so much I need to learn; even just starting is overwhelming.

- I am a busy person with no time. Or others need me, and I hide in service for others rather than taking care of me.

- If I succeed, I may be judged for my choices by family or friends.

- It did not work the first time I tried, so it was not meant for me.

- I do not have a support system for the project.

- I'll need more money to accomplish it, or I do not know how much money I will need.

- I'm procrastinating. It's easier to scroll through social media, sleep, and make myself busy.

When you have identified what is stopping you, you have the agency to make a decision. Is it really a goal? Or is it a wish that sounds good, but you are unwilling to do the work to obtain it? Or is it a *should*, meaning someone else's dream you think you should want too? One of the most critical decisions and course corrections is deciding not to work toward a financial goal because it is really not important to you! The longer you let it linger, the more you tell yourself you want it but still do not act on it, the more it becomes a burden of guilt.

Wishing you did something is much harder over time than actually doing the work, even if you fail. If you fail, you learn—*next*! In our home, I often say that *next* is my favorite four-letter word. When we fail, we learn what did not work, and we try again. *Next*. Truth be told, I do like to cuss a little, too, so I have many favorite four-letter words, but this one is the most productive. *Next!*

> Wishing you did something is much harder over time than actually doing the work, even if you fail.

Further Reflections

- Do you have negative thoughts that keep you from having money confidence?

- Do you have financial course corrections you need to consider?

- From what do you need to move on?

Money Smarts

- You can significantly impact your financial confidence by aligning your money with your dreams and desires.

- Do not lose sight of your long-term financial goals by reacting without a plan for a short-term change in circumstances.

- What you think your key desires are may be what you have told yourself or what someone else has told you you *should* feel.

- The longer you let financial changes linger, the more the situation becomes a burden of guilt. Wishing you did something is much harder over time than actually doing the work, even if you fail.

CHAPTER 14

Money Smarts: The Bottom Line

Money is emotional, period. If you think you
are 100 percent logical about it all the time,
you are not being truthful with yourself.

—Hal Neibling

W hen I was thirteen, my dad, Harold Neibling, started my lessons in what he called Money Smarts. My father's perspective was unique because he taught me about behavioral finance—what people do with their money and why. In the early 1980s, this was an unusual approach. He taught me about the emotions that surround money and how they impact our happiness with money. These were big concepts for a thirteen-year-old, but they kindled my deep interest in behavioral finance, ultimately leading me to my life's work.

He was a bottom-line man who loved a good story, but in the end, he would ask me, "What is the lesson?" In his honor, the following are all the key learnings I hope you will take from this book, in a bullet-point format. While each of the chapters contain the examples and stories needed to help you understand the concepts in a more meaningful and nuanced way, here is the bottom line.

Part I: The Basics of Behavioral Finance

Chapter 1: What Are Money Wounds and Why Do They Matter?

- Money wounds are negative experiences or memories we have around money that impact our current relationship with it.
- The most common causes of financial scar tissue (lingering memories or habits from wounds) are expectations, regret, fear, shame, power, and control.

Chapter 2: Behavioral Finance versus Traditional Finance

- Behavioral finance is what we do, consciously and unconsciously, because of our experiences with money.
- Each of us has our unique mix of emotions, blind spots, and influences that can radically change our outcomes with money.
- Money scripts are our unconscious beliefs around money.
- Money biases are our habitual responses to money.
- Money disorders go from mild to severe and can be as destructive as other addictions.

Chapter 3: The Social Media Game-Changer

- Social media has created an online currency of likes, influencers, and curated imagery.

- With financial decisions often based on emotion, social media's influence is a game-changer.

- Clean up your social media feed so you don't see posts that may cause you to compare yourself financially or influence unnecessary purchases.

- Investment advice through a social media scroll is an advertisement, not a hot tip!

Chapter 4: Aligning Your Money and Values

- We only reach money satisfaction when we know what we value.

- Values reflect your own assessments of what is important in your life and with your money.

- To take control of your financial life, you must determine what you value without judgment or shame.

Chapter 5: Financial Wounds and Their Origins

- Wounds often come from deep-seated beliefs that we absorb from our families, communities, or cultural backgrounds.

- Identifying your wounds is to remind yourself that they are not a permanent part of your financial life.

- Financial wounds cause pain because they do not align with our personal desires.

- Financial negativity often comes from fear and disappointment in an unexamined financial life.

Chapter 6: Planning for Your Goals

- Identify your most important money goals.
- Know why your financial goals are important; challenge the why behind each goal.
- Enlist your partner, a coach, or a financial advisor to help you stay on track with your stated desires.

Part II: Building Your Financial Foundation

Chapter 7: Cost of Living

- The key to planning is understanding what it costs you to live monthly and annually.
- Understand what type of expenses you have—both discretionary and fixed costs. Is your financial spending in alignment with your goals?
- By establishing what you spend to live, you can more accurately plan for financial goals.
- Ignorance is not bliss! Freedom can be found in understanding your cost of living.

Chapter 8: Cash Reserves and Debt Management

- Keep money simple by reducing, eliminating, or never having high consumer debt levels and maintaining a cash reserve for unexpected moments.

- When you have a lack of cash reserves and mounting debt, that is a sign that your monthly spending may be beyond your means.

- Most people who carry a lot of debt and are trying to pay it down will take *all* their discretionary income and try to put as much as they can toward paying down their bills. This can create a debt loop; there is a better way.

Chapter 9: Protection Planning

- Plan for the certainty of uncertainty.

- Protection planning is a formal way to plan for catastrophic life events that could derail your financial plans and deplete your savings.

- Protecting your risk in the areas of health care, disability, life, and long-term-care coverage may be vital to securing the financial future you desire for yourself and your family.

Chapter 10: Putting Your Money to Work

- Wealth is typically built by investing over time, with your short-term needs liquid and your long-term money invested in the risk tolerance you can handle when markets decline.

- Investing involves buying financial assets that have the potential to grow in value while managing risk in alignment with your goals and time horizon.

- Diversification is dividing your assets into different asset classes to minimize risk.

- The key is to educate yourself on the risks and the different types of vehicles that are available.

- **WARNING:** There are many types of investments, and they all carry various levels of risk. Always know what you are investing in, why you are investing in a particular vehicle, and what the historical returns are. This falls under the adage "There are no dumb questions." If someone is making you feel that way, *run*! Do *not* invest with them.

Chapter 11: What Is Your Money Legacy?

- Your financial legacy is how you leave your money when you die.

- Estate planning is essential for leaving a healthy money legacy.

- Estate planning is not just for distribution of assets after death. It can also address how medical and financial decisions are made for you when you are unable to do so.

- Please consider working with an estate planning attorney to review your current document or create new documents in alignment with your values.

Chapter 12: Habits and Resilience

- How you interact and think about your money is often so deeply entrenched in your habits that it's hard to change your thoughts and behaviors.

- Money is emotional. Developing resilience and understanding how you feel, think, and interact with money is the golden key to true financial success.

Chapter 13: Confidence and Course Corrections

- You can significantly impact your financial confidence by aligning your money with your dreams and desires.

- Do not lose sight of your long-term financial goals by reacting without a plan for a short-term change in circumstances.

- What you think your key desires are may be what you have told yourself or what someone else has told you you *should* feel.

- The longer you let financial changes linger, the more the situation becomes a burden of guilt. Wishing you did something is much harder over time than actually doing the work, even if you fail.

Thrive

My mission in life is not merely to
survive but to thrive and to do so with some
passion, compassion, humor, and style.

—Maya Angelou

The greatest joy I experience professionally is when someone walks into my office frightened, anxious, or unsure about their financial future and walks out with peace of mind. Not all financial issues can be solved in an hour-long meeting, but just laying it all out and talking candidly about money can create a profound shift in our destructive self-talk.

When you focus your brain on one single thing like money, you can start to obsess about it. You worry, don't sleep, become anxious, and are not so nice to yourself or others. Many of us ruminate on money because it is critical to our survival—and we believe that money is how society judges us.

I wrote this book to show you what causes you to go to these dark places around money and to put you on the path to peace of mind. It is really a very simple process, but it's not always easy. You may need to make some tough decisions, and your family dynamics around money may be challenged. It may not be comfortable—do it anyway.

Many people in the world live in such poverty or oppressive conditions that they do not have control over their financial lives. The rest of us do. We give up that control when we allow emotional responses driven by our fears, regrets, and ideas about other people's thoughts to shape our current financial reality.

I hope you choose to use the tools and insights in this book to reshape those emotions, grant yourself the agency to change your circumstances, and *thrive*!

With love and absolute belief in you that you can identify and learn to thrive with your financial wounds,

—Shannon

Acknowledgments

Behavioral finance has been my passion since I was thirteen years old. Working with real people and their money has been an incredible journey, and I am excited to share what I've learned with a broader audience. First and foremost, I want to thank my husband, Chris, and our daughters, Lauren and Taylor, for their unwavering support of my dream.

To my sisters, Lisa and Kristin, thank you for always being my foundation and sounding board. Your wisdom and love have been invaluable to me. Thank you to my family, friends, and the Ryan Wealth team for letting me run ideas by you and supporting this book, even though I've talked your ear off about it. Your patience and encouragement have meant the world to me.

Tom, Emily, Heather, and Eliza, your belief in this project, your insights, and your gentle nudging to keep going have made all the difference. Thank you for helping me "push through" and complete this project.

Notes

Chapter 1

1. *Oxford English Dictionary*, "regret," accessed February 6, 2025, https://www.oed.com/dictionary/regret_n?tl=true.

2. "Gen X Approaching Retirement Crunch Time with Savings Regrets," Allianz, June 13, 2024, https://www.allianzlife.com/about/newsroom/2024-Press-Releases/Gen-X-Approaching-Retirement-Crunch-Time-with-Savings-Regrets.

3. Tiffany Curtis, "How Generational Trauma Affects Your Finances and How to Heal," NerdWallet, November 2, 2022, https://www.nerdwallet.com/article/finance/generational-trauma.

4. Amanda Albright, "Fearful Millennials Missed Stock Market Rally with Shift to Cash," *Bloomberg*, April 24, 2023, https://www.bloomberg.com/news/articles/2023-04-24/stock-market-investing-mistakes-millennials-shifted-to-cash-in-timing-blunder.

5. "AARP Report Finds $28.3 Billion a Year Is Stolen from U.S. Adults over 60," AARP Press Room, June 15, 2023, https://press.aarp.org/2023-06-15-AARP-Report-Finds-28-Billion-a-Year-is-Stolen-from-US-Adults-Over-60.

6. Federal Trade Commission, "Protecting Older Consumers 2022–2023: A Report of the Federal Trade Commission," October 2023, https://www.ftc.gov/reports/protecting-older-consumers-2022-2023-report-federal-trade-commission.

Chapter 2

1. Alessandro Baroni, "Financial Literacy Ranking by Country," Sweat Your Assets, February 21, 2022, https://sweatyourassets.biz/financial-literacy-ranking-by-country.

2. Baroni, "Financial Literacy Ranking by Country."

3. Brad Klontz, Rick Kahler, and Ted Klontz, *Facilitating Financial Health: Tools for Financial Planners, Coaches, and Therapists* (National Underwriter Company, 2016), 34.

4. Klontz et al., *Facilitating Financial Health*, 77–79.

5. Eva M. Krockow, "How Many Decisions Do We Make Each Day?," *Psychology Today*, September 27, 2018, https://www.psychologytoday.com/us/blog/stretching-theory/201809/how-many-decisions-do-we-make-each-day.

6. Daniel Kahneman and Amos Tversky, "Prospect Theory: An Analysis of Decision Under Risk," *Econometrica* 47, no. 2 (1979): 263–291, https://doi.org/10.2307/1914185.

7. Bradley Klontz, Sonya L. Britt, Kristy L. Archuleta, and Ted Klontz, "Disordered Money Behaviors: Development of the Klontz Money Behavior Inventory," *Journal of Financial Therapy* 3, no. 1 (2012): 95–97, https://doi.org/10.4148/jft.v3i1.1485.

8. Klontz et al., *Facilitating Financial Health*, 94–95.

Chapter 3

1. Trevor Haynes, "Dopamine, Smartphones & You: A Battle for Your Time," Harvard University, May 1, 2018, https://unplugged.sunygeneseoenglish.org/wp-content/uploads/sites/31/2019/11/Domamine-PDF.pdf.

2. Pesala Bandara, "Instagram and TikTok Hurt Happiness and Finances, Survey Finds," PetaPixel, July 19, 2022, https://petapixel.com/2022 /07/19/instagram-and-tiktok-hurt-happiness-and-finances-survey -finds/.

3. Serena Espeute and Rhodri G. Preece, "The Finfluencer Appeal: Investing in the Age of Social Media," CFA Institute, January 25, 2024, https://rpc.cfainstitute.org/en/research/reports/2024/finfluencer-appeal.

Chapter 4

1. Patty Kreamer, "Align Yourself with Your Needs and Values," Financial Planning Association, June 2020, https://www.financialplanning association.org/article/align-yourself-your-needs-and-values.

2. "Starting Early for Financial Success: Capability into Action," *The Journal of Consumer Affairs* 49, no. 1 (Spring 2015), 299–302, https:// doi.org/10.1111/joca.12063.

3. *Cambridge Dictionary*, "values," accessed February 6, 2025, https:// dictionary.cambridge.org/us/dictionary/english/values#google_vignette.

4. Oliver Stone, director, *Wall Street*, 20th Century Fox, 1987.

5. Oliver Stone, director, *Wall Street*, 20th Century Fox, 1987.

Chapter 5

1. Annamaria Lusardi and Olivia S. Mitchell, "Baby Boomer Retirement Security: The Roles of Planning, Financial Literacy, and Housing Wealth" *Journal of Monetary Economics* 54, no. 1 (2007): 205–224, https://doi.org/10.1016/j.jmoneco.2006.12.001.

Chapter 6

1. Bill George, *True North: Discover Your Authentic Leadership* (Jossey-Bass, 2007).

Chapter 7

1. "Upside to Inflation: More Americans Are Budgeting Today Than Ever Before," PR Newswire, April 27, 2022, https://www.prnewswire.com /news-releases/upside-to-inflation-more-americans-are-budgeting -than-ever-before-301533720.html.

2. "Social Desirability Bias in Psychology: Definition, Effects, and Implications," NeuroLaunch, September 14, 2024, https://neurolaunch .com/social-desirability-bias-psychology-definition/.

Chapter 8

1. Lane Gillespie, "Bankrate's 2025 Annual Emergency Savings Report," Bankrate, January 23, 2025, https://www.bankrate.com/banking /savings/emergency-savings-report.

2. Matt Schulz, "49% of Americans Can't Afford a $1,000 Emergency, with Many Relying on Credit Cards for Unexpected Expenses," LendingTree, December 11, 2023, https://www.lendingtree.com /debt-consolidation/emergency-savings-survey.

Chapter 9

1. T. Smith and D. Lee, "The State of Insurance Coverage in America: Trends, Gaps, and Policy Solutions," *Journal of Health Economics and Policy* 48, no. 2 (2024): 202–217.

Chapter 10

1. "More Than Half of Teens Think Investing Is Too Confusing: Fidelity Shares Resources to Help Parents Have 'The Talk,'" Business Wire, June 7, 2022, https://www.businesswire.com/news/home/20220607005350 /en/More-Than-Half-of-Teens-Think-Investing-Is-Too-Confusing -Fidelity-Shares-Resources-to-Help-Parents-Have-%E2%80%9C The-Talk%E2%80%9D.

2. "Citizens Survey Finds Majority of Americans Ill-Prepared for Historic Multigenerational Wealth Transfer," Citizens Financial Group, May 15,

2024, https://investor.citizensbank.com/about-us/newsroom/latest
-news/2024/2024-05-15-140037162.aspx.

3. Kaisa S. Pietikäinen, "Misunderstandings and Ensuring Understanding
in Private ELF Talk," *Applied Linguistics* 39, no. 2 (2018): 188–212,
https://doi.org/10.1093/applin/amw005.

Chapter 11

1. Rachel Lustbader, "2024 Wills and Estate Planning Study," Caring.
com, July 30, 2024, https://www.caring.com/caregivers/estate-planning
/wills-survey.

Chapter 12

1. Shannon Ryan, "Confronting Your Financial Scar Tissue," TEDx Talks,
May 19, 2022, 15:40, https://youtu.be/LtQBW2hCDYc?si=s_CY
-HS76-xKYOL.

2. James Clear, "How Long Does It Actually Take to Form a New Habit?
(Backed by Science)," JamesClear.com, https://jamesclear.com
/new-habit.

3. American Psychological Association, "Resilience," APA.org, accessed
September 13, 2024, https://www.apa.org/topics/resilience.

4. Mei-Chung Rosemary Lin, "Resilience and Financial Well-Being:
Money Attitudes as Mediator," *US-China Education Review* 12, no. 2
(2022), DOI:10.17265/2161-623X/2022.02.001.

Chapter 13

1. Rachel Carey, "Financial Confidence in the US," Unbiased, November
27, 2024, https://www.unbiased.com/discover/financial-advice
/financial-confidence-in-the-us.

2. Jeff Grabmeier, "More People Confident They Know Finances—
Despite the Evidence," Ohio State News, September 8, 2022,
https://news.osu.edu/more-people-confident-they-know-finances
--despite-the-evidence.

Index

About
the Author

Shannon Ryan, CFP®, is a veteran in the financial services industry with more than thirty years of experience. She is known for her deep passion for financial literacy, ignited by her father's "Money Smarts" when she was thirteen. These early lessons laid the foundation for her interest in the behavioral and emotional aspects of money management. Shannon's unique approach stems from her real-world experience guiding individuals and families through life's financial ups and downs, making her advice practical and relatable.

In addition to being a Certified Financial Planner, Shannon is a sought-after public speaker, having delivered a TEDx Talk and made numerous media appearances. Her platform, *The Heavy Purse*, offers a variety of resources designed to make financial education accessible, including blogs, vlogs, and coaching materials. Shannon emphasizes starting financial literacy conversations and empowering people to make sound money decisions.

Her work makes complex financial concepts easy to understand, helping people navigate money's emotional landscape. She is also a proud mom of two daughters and a wife married to her college sweetheart, living in a community they love.

www.TheHeavyPurse.com